Praise for "Nanny to the Rescue Again!

"Michelle LaRowe has done it again. *Nanny to the Rescue Again!* offers parents of every faith simple and practical tips on dealing with the everyday, yet incredibly frustrating, challenges we all face. Michelle speaks in a voice that is honest, yet respectful, and conveys her message with compassion and humor. In a world that has never been more chaotic or confusing, this book should be required reading for all parents."

> Jim Taylor, PhD
> Author of *Your Children are Under Attack: How Popular Culture is Destroying Your Kids' Values and How You Can Protect Them*

"Michelle LaRowe changes what we think about the stereotypical nanny. Young, hip, and educated, she is witty, funny, pretty, and most importantly, incredibly well-versed in her answers to any question when it comes to children. Got a question, any question, Michelle has an answer that makes perfect sense in a no-nonsense approach that works."

> Jon Griffin
> Host and Producer, Coffee Roundtable
> Cumulus Radio Dallas

"Contagious, energetic, and a really fast talker, Michelle LaRowe is a professional, confident woman with a passion for her work. LaRowe passes on that confidence, along with practical parenting tips, to moms and dads of school-aged kids."

> Sue Goldie, MD, MPH
> Harvard School of Public Health
> Department of Health Policy and Management

"She's done it again! Michelle LaRowe helps us through the difficult spots of parenting and gives us practical tips to build a positive family life. *Nanny to the Rescue Again!* provides the boost parents need through the grade-school years in order to raise godly, respectful children. This is an essential reference tool for every mom and dad."

> Karol Ladd
> Author of *Power of a Positive Mom*
> and the *Positive Plan* series

"*Nanny to the Rescue Again!* is an impressive guidebook for moms, dads, and caregivers. I've seen many books that tell parents how to potty train but few that teach them how to help their kids respond to school bullies and peer pressure. It will really help parents know what their kids need from them during that time."

Kelly McCausey
Mom's Radio Network

"Michelle is a true expert. Her passion leaps off the page with anecdotes and lessons from her own experience as a career nanny making this book a must-have for parents and caretakers."

Samantha Ettus
Creator of *The Expert's Guide to the Baby Years*

"Michelle's positive and calming attitude truly speaks from experience and her scenarios add a real life personality easy to relate to. This book offers parents the perfect balance of clear, straight-forward advice, and strong, practical support."

Cheryl Tallman
CEO and Co-founder, Fresh Baby

"*Nanny to the Rescue Again!* picks up where the first book left off, when you're preparing your kiddos for school, and sending them off to learn to fly solo. Michelle approaches every situation in a loving, practical way using her ten-plus-years of experience as a nanny to explain the (relatively) simple processes. No doubt about it, you'll be a better parent after reading this book!"

Susan J. Alt
Editor-in-Chief, *TWINS*™ Magazine

"There is a tremendous amount of good advice. It provides concrete methods and tips for parents including adjusting to school, doing homework, and meeting new playmates. A must-read for parents with school-age children!"

Geraldine Jensen, Editor
Families Online Magazine

"Tired of feeling like your kids are driving the car? Michelle LaRowe puts parents back in the driver's seat. Her ideas for dealing with school-aged kids are not only wise—they work. If you have kids you need this book!"

Chuck Borsellion, PhD, PsyD
Author of *Pinocchio Parenting*

MICHELLE R. LAROWE

nanny TO THE RESCUE AGAIN!

W PUBLISHING GROUP
A Division of Thomas Nelson Publishers
Since 1798

www.wpublishinggroup.com

Published by W Publishing Group, a division of Thomas Nelson, Inc., P.O. Box 141000, Nashville, TN 37214.

The author is represented by the literary agency of WordServe Literary Group, 10152 S. Knoll Circle, Highlands Ranch, CO 80130.

Unless otherwise marked, all Scripture quotations are taken from the Holy Bible, New International Version®. Copyright © 1973, 1978, 1984 by International Bible Society. Used by permission of Zondervan. All rights reserved. Scriptures marked YLT are taken from Young's Literal Translation. Public domain. Scriptures marked TLB are taken from The Living Bible. Copyright © 1971 by Tyndale House Publishers, Wheaton, Ill. Used by permission. All rights reserved.

Library of Congress Cataloging-in-Publication Data

LaRowe, Michelle R.
   Nanny to the rescue again! : straight talk and super tips for parents of grade-schoolers / Michelle LaRowe.
      p. cm.
   Includes bibliographical references.
   ISBN-13: 978-0-8499-1244-3
   ISBN-10: 0-8499-1244-X
  1. Child rearing. 2. Parenting. 3. Parent and child. 4. School children.
I. Title.
  HQ769.L2495 2006
  649'.124—dc22   2006024020

Printed in the United States of America
06 07 08 09 RRD 9 8 7 6 5 4 3 2 1

CONTENTS

SECTION THREE   Help for the Home Front

*To my mom,
who always comes to my rescue*

ACKNOWLEDGMENTS

God doesn't call the equipped; He equips the called.

Thank You, Lord.
When I said I'd go, You said You'd send me.
When I thought I wasn't good enough, You reminded me, "But I AM."
When I was scared I didn't have the preparation, You prepared me.
When man closed windows, You opened doors.
Amen.

Greg and Becky Johnson—As the Lord always completes what He starts, so do you! Your zealousness for this project, your grace for my learning curve, and your unconditional love for me and "Nanny" have again brought us to the completion of another successful project. Thank you.

Debbie Wickwire—I'm so glad to have met you in person! What an inspiration you have been to our team. Your hands-on role in this project has made it as smooth as silk and practically perfect in every way!

Kristin Mullenix—Thank you for your commitment and dedication to this project. I've grown quite fond of you and your family and enjoy reading about your daily joys of parenting. I especially love hearing how my tips "really do work!" You really know your PR stuff. Thanks for teaching me the ropes.

Jennifer Stair—We give new meaning to "all in a day's work." Thanks for the tag-team effort! Like I say, a team of two is always better than two teams of one!

Team W—Thanks for all your work. I hope you're as proud of me as I am of representing you.

Mom—Love ya. What else is there to say?

Boys—The distance between our homes is never a measure of the distance between our hearts. I love you both dearly.

Pastors Joe and Donna Sapienza—Thanks for all your love, guidance, support, encouragement, and occasional correction. Thanks for always covering me in prayer.

The pastoral staff at Celebration International Church—I am blessed. I am thinking about you.

Sharon—Your daily prayers have power. You're faithful to your word. Thanks.

All my CIC family—You truly are my family. Thanks.

My friends and family—You are all gems. Thanks for your patience with me and my schedule. Although space may have separated us during my time with this project, you were all never far from my heart. Thanks for all your love and understanding.

My "family"—Thank you for giving me the opportunity to love your children and become a special part of your family. I'm grateful for your support and encouragement in my writing projects.

INTRODUCTION

Today is the big day. You send your first child off to school in his starched new clothes, with his spiffy lunch box, and wearing a backpack that makes him look like an adorable walking turtle. You walk him to the bus stop and envision the happy times to come: spending evenings helping your growing child sound out words in his *See Jane Run* primer, practicing the multiplication table with your third grader, and sharing the fun of his pint-sized academic world.

"School days, school days, dear old golden rule days."

There's nothing like the joy of hearing all about what your child has learned in school!

Or not.

Because the truth is, what kids learn in kindergarten today may not be exactly what you dreamed about. If it hasn't happened already, you may soon observe behavior or hear words you are certain your child didn't learn at home. You may even find yourself thinking, *Whose kid is he?*

Has "Nobody Likes Me, Everybody Hates Me" become your children's theme song?

Does their homework load have you tearing out your hair?

Do you find yourself embroiled in arguments with no visible sign of escape?

If so, welcome to the world of grade-schoolers.

Maybe you've experienced a conversation with your second grader that went something like this:

JOEY. Mom, can I watch the new Lord of the Rings movie?
MOM. No, honey, I don't think so.
JOEY. Why not?

MOM. It's PG-13, and you are not thirteen.

JOEY. Kevin watched it, and he's not thirteen.

MOM. Well, if Kevin jumped off a bridge, would you do it too?

JOEY. I would if I had a parachute.

MOM. That's beside the point; you are too young to see the movie.

JOEY. I could get a fake ID, like Mike's buddy.

MOM. Oh my goodness. Where did you hear about fake IDs?

Pretty soon you are longing for a parachute so you can safely jump out of these tug-of-war conversations.

Chances are if you're holding this book in your hands right now, you have survived the first years of your child's life, hopefully with few, if any, physical, emotional, or psychological casualties to yourself, your spouse, or your child. I know that's the case if we're old friends and you applied some of the tricks of the nanny trade that I shared in my first book, *Nanny to the Rescue!*[1] If not, no worries. You are here now, and if you absorb my straight talk and super tips for grade-schoolers in this book, you'll be a practically perfect parent in no time at all.

OK, maybe I'm promising a bit too much. After all, no parent can be perfect. However, I do promise to give you three things in this book: an informative and enjoyable read, ideas that can increase your confidence and effectiveness as a parent, and techniques that will improve your kids' behavior and outlook on school, home, and life in general.

Nanny to the Rescue Again! picks up where the first book stopped: at the doors of your local elementary school, covering ages six through twelve (or first grade though sixth grade).

As a professional nanny with more than a decade of experience, I've had the unique opportunity to observe families transition their little ones into the grade-school years. I've seen parents grieve as they are suddenly left home alone all day, their job description now radically altered. (Of course, I've also seen mothers—usually of multiples—nearly dance a freedom jig as they walked their youngest child to the door on the first day of school.) I know what it's like to feel angered and saddened for a child who is being bullied at school or facing malicious rumors passed along the gossip grapevine. I've also shared the astonishment as I've witnessed a young charge's vocabulary grow by leaps and bounds—but not always in the way I, or his parents, would have liked.

The good news is that even with the obstacles ahead, the middle years of childhood are generally the most enjoyable for parents. There's no experience quite like the pride of watching your opera-star-to-be belting out "Twinkle, Twinkle Little Star" with an earnest lisp at her first spring concert. And the first time your son reads a book by himself, your heart will skip a beat as you share in his excitement.

You'll softly laugh at the whispers of little girls planning their futures and little boys sharing their dreams of batting in the big leagues. And you'll experience that odd mixture of sorrow and pride the first time your child proudly announces that she no longer needs you to accompany her to the bus or into her classroom.

The first season of parenting is one where you bundle, cuddle, and stay on high alert as you guard your baby from the minefields of the common home: electric outlets, sharp corners, breakables on coffee tables, and the ever-popular insect snacks. (Why is it that we can't get babies to eat their green peas, but if allowed, they'll search every corner of the house to find and scarf down a dead bug?)

If a child is to keep his inborn sense of wonder. . . he needs the companionship of at least one adult who can share it, rediscovering with him the joy, excitement and mystery of the world we live in.
—Rachel Carson

The grade-school season of parenting is when the winds begin, ever so slowly, to shift toward independence. It is a time when you have to learn to let go and trust the values you've instilled in your children to be their anchor in the world. A time when you must learn to trust that things will be OK, that you have done your job well. You will still be there to protect your child, just not always in the same ways. During these grade-school years, it helps to think of yourself as the Great Preparer, readying your child for a successful debut into a healthy, confident, and loving adulthood.

So grab your number-two pencil and your Big Chief tablet for notes, and let's start our first parenting lesson, shall we? (I might even give out a few gold stars . . .)

SECTION
ONE

YOU BROUGHT THIS CHILD INTO THE WORLD . . . NOW YOU HAVE TO LET HIM GO

(YIKES!)

CHAPTER ONE

SEParaTING WITH SANITY

 ### Scene 1: Take 1
The First Day of School

MOM. It's going to be OK, Zachary. You'll have a great first day of school. *(Her voice quivers, and her smile is weak.)*

ZACH, *nonchalantly.* Yup! I can't wait! *(He walks into school with a spring in his step.)*

MOM, *following close behind, trying to keep up with her son.* How about a hug and a kiss for Mommy?

ZACH. Mom, you don't have to walk me inside, you know. I know where my classroom is. *(He blows a kiss her in direction and turns to greet his friends with a smile.)*

MOM, *fighting off the tears.* OK, honey, I'll pick you up right outside at three o'clock.

ZACH. OK! Bye, Mom!

MOM, *turns and slowly exits the school building. Then spying a group of other moms chatting out front, she joins them.* Why do they have to grow up so fast? I never thought the day would come that he wouldn't need me, never mind want me!

SECOND MOM, *moving to console her*. Sooner or later, all mothers experience this moment of no longer feeling needed by their kids. Today appears to be your day. It's a bit of a shock, isn't it?
(Unable to form the words through the lump in her throat, Zach's mom simply nods.)

The most important thing that parents can teach their children is how to get along without them.
—Frank A. Clark

Whether your day has come or is soon approaching—indeed, someday the realization hits: you and your child are two independent people who are in the process of learning to function without being attached at the hip. Since you literally carried the little tykes inside your womb, then in your arms, followed by years of having the pitter-patter of their feet right behind yours, it's no wonder that something as simple as dropping them off at school can feel like an amputation of sorts! No matter how much you might have wished for a few hours of alone time, there's a transition period where most moms feel a real loss. And it's especially potent with the first and last child!

In parenting, there is the physical game and the mental game. The physical game is running through the actions. The mental game is running them through in your head.
—Michelle LaRowe

Long gone are the days of spoon-feeding your toddler or tying your preschooler's shoes. If you've done your job well, your child started with, "I can do it myself!" and has now begun saying, "I don't want you to walk me into school today; I'm a big boy." It's bittersweet, isn't it? We want them to fly, and yet . . . we miss having them next to us, safe in the nest.

Getting Kids Ready for the Big Leagues

It seems like just yesterday you were holding your child's hands as he learned to steadily walk the length of a field. He needed you to support him, to pick him up when he fell down. But it's a new game now. You are no longer playing backyard ball, where you can run in and call a time-out anytime you choose. Your job, at this point, is to cheer your little batter as he steps up to the plate. You can't hold his hands as he swings at the ball. (Well, you could, but your child would suffer untold embarrassment by his peers for the rest of his school life.)

He has to try; he must let the proverbial ball fly fair (or foul) on his own. You can, however, observe the play (the good, the bad, and the ugly) and take mental notes. Once the game is over—and when your child is receptive and asks for comments—you can encourage and advise.

All healthy parents gradually move from the role of a full-time, hands-on coach to more of a consultant and comforter. It doesn't happen all at once, thank goodness. And your children will always love and need you at some level for the rest of their lives.

Nanny Tip

Your kids are looking to you to see how they should respond to situations. If you have a positive attitude, they will too. If you embrace change easily, so will your children!

Practice Will Pay Off

The ultimate goal of good parenting is to equip your children with the knowledge, life skills, and confidence to make healthy choices. As parents, you want to train your kids so their default behavior is kind, wise, compassionate, and fair—whether or not you are watching. A tall order, you say? Yep, it is. And of course, your child will try and fail and then get back in the game and try again . . . many times. Growing up isn't easy for any of us. But without the testing ground of real life, most of us would not have matured. The playground is a laboratory for real life. It is where we learned cooperation on a seesaw, how to handle (or avoid) bullies, and how to go down a slide without getting burned.

If you've done your job well to this point (and most parents who care enough to read a book on parenting are in that category), do not fear: your child will enter her elementary-school years with your voice in her ear. I'm an adult, and I still hear my mother's voice in my head whenever I'm tempted to go in a counterproductive direction! I bet you do too. (I have a friend who tells me she even hears her mother whisper, "Get the double rolls; it saves time and money in the long run!" when she's shopping for toilet paper and tempted to go the cheap route.)

 ### *Nanny Tip*

Here are ten key elements that will provide your child with comfort and stability during life transitions:

1. Family support
2. Friends
3. Rest, exercise, and healthy food
4. Prayer
5. Laughter
6. Gathering and sorting information
7. Keeping a healthy sense of fun and adventure
8. Being patient with your child (and teaching him to be patient with himself)
9. Maintaining consistency where you can
10. Taking a time-out for yourself

By incorporating these elements into your child's days, settling into a new normal will start to feel more fun and exciting than scary and worrisome.

So although you may not hold your child's physical hand as she experiences life outside your home, you certainly hold her heart—and the memories of your words of wisdom, love, prayer, and discipline go with her into every circumstance.

Putting On Your Game Face

In the opening scene of the first day of school, it was obvious that this mother felt more insecure than her child. You may be nervous about all your child may encounter in this new world, but to borrow a phrase from a deodorant commercial, "Never let 'em see you sweat". Portray a positive, confident attitude about your child's transition to school (or any other major life transition), and it will impact the way your child embraces the change.

I'm gonna let you in on a little secret: I don't like change. I like waking up at the same time each morning, arriving at work at the same time and at the same place, and leaving work at a consistent hour each night. That's been my routine for the past seven years, and it soothes my inner Mary Poppins. I enjoy knowing that on Sunday mornings and Wednesday evenings I'll be at church and that Saturday night is girls' night out. I take comfort in knowing that each May I take my vacation. For as long as I can remember, I've loved words like *schedule* and *organization* and *planning*. I get warm fuzzies over planners and date books and calendars. I brake for The Container Store.

I am nearing the third decade of an ordered life, and I don't like when a wrench is thrown into my dependable routine. But recently, I have been going through lots of transitions and changes in a short amount of time. Even though most of them are good things, there are still lots of new experiences happening all at once, which makes me especially empathetic with kids coping with the shift from Mom's familiar kitchen to the crowded kindergarten cafeteria.

My recent experience has been helpful for me in terms of feeling empathy for anyone in transition: whether a child going off to school for the first time or a mother adjusting to another phase of life. What helped me during the shaky transitional phase may also be of help to you and your child.

Preparing Your Child for School

Here are some ways you might keep your child feeling centered as he goes off to school or any new place, based on my personal experience and information from other parents and child experts. These small activities take just a moment of time but pay enormous dividends in terms of peace and confidence as your child faces new challenges.

Practice your child's new schedule. For example, a week before school starts, begin waking up and going to bed on school time. Lay out clothes the night before so morning time is less stressed, and then do some trial runs for fun. On one of the days, do a school drill—see if your child can get dressed and ready: bed made, teeth brushed, backpack loaded, and ready to go by a certain time on a preset alarm. Then instead of going to school (since it won't yet be open!), go out for a celebration pancake breakfast.

Do some information gathering with your child. Let him ask you questions, and share with him what to expect at school. Help him deal with any fears or concerns, such as, "What if I lose my lunch money?" or "How will I get home?"

Role-play situations that are bound to come up during the school day. For example, to prepare him for when he needs to use the bathroom in the middle of class but is not sure what to do, you say, "Zach, if you need to use the bathroom during class, raise your hand high for the teacher to see, and when she calls on you, ask if you can use the bathroom." Then say, "OK, Zach? I'll pretend to be the teacher. Now show me what you do when you need to go to the bathroom."

Teach him what to do when he doesn't know what to do. "Speak up! If you have a question, ask it! But raise your hand first and ask politely. Most likely someone else has the same question too."

Go over the school rules together. Most schools provide a handbook, so be sure to review it with your child. Highlight what you feel will really affect your child.

Try to get together with at least one other student before the first day of school. Most schools provide a class list toward the end of the summer. Plan a picnic at the school playground so that your child can make a new friend.

Attend school events. Many schools have a "meet and greet" day before school begins, a time to meet your child's teacher and other classmates. Take advantage of these opportunities.

Make fun events of shopping for school supplies and school clothes. Let your child handle and sort his supplies and pack them in his backpack. Ask him what special treats he might like to have in his lunch box the first week of school, and try to provide one or two of them.

Pray for your child. If you are comfortable with prayer, casually pray for your child before he goes to school, maybe even as you drive (with your eyes open!), and make the prayer full of anticipation and hope. ("Lord, I thank You for letting my child be such a special boy at home, and I ask that You show him how he can be a blessing to his friends and teacher today. We trust You to make it a good day!")

Assure him that God is with him everywhere and that he can talk to God anytime. When he's old enough to read, put a verse of Scripture or a loving thought or a funny joke in his lunch box. Before he's ready to read, draw a fun picture or cartoon to tuck into his backpack or lunch box. My mom taught me to wake up each day shouting, "Hey, Lord, I'm glad I'm alive! Thank You for another day, and send help. I'll need it all day long." Thirty years later, I still follow that routine, and it not only gets me out of bed but gets me out on the *right* side of the bed.

I know another woman (now in her sixties) who told me that her hardworking but ever-positive single mother put her feet over the side of her bed every morning and cheerfully said aloud, "I get to go to work today!" Can you imagine what that attitude would do for children?

Now They Are Happily Off to School, but What About You?

Now you have the tools to get your child pumped and ready to tackle her first day of school. Congratulations. Now what about you? If you are a working mom, you already know how you'll be filling your days. However, you may have to work out details of getting your kids to school and possibly after-school care.

If you are a stay-at-home mom and don't have other kids at home to care for, how can you ease your mind and transition to more hours in your day apart from your child? Yes, I know many of you moms have wisely and excitedly been planning how to fill up this free time for years. (Guilt-free naps! Lunching out where they don't give plastic toys in paper bags!) But lots of mothers have simply been so busy, well . . . *mothering*, they've not had time to think about life after school starts.

How can you develop a plan to tackle the transition? Plan a new fall schedule for yourself. After your child or children are off to school, you could schedule a morning walk. Going with another mom with whom you can share the joys and struggles you are enountering. Plan lunch dates with your friends. Volunteer for a local organization. Go to the gym—you know, the one you belong to but could never make time for before now? Take a class, find a hobby, read a book, or re-organize that closet you haven't had time to do. If you've dreamed of completing your college degree and there are no more little ones at home, this is the perfect time to go back to school. Start slowly, taking only three to six class hours, to see how much extra stress it will be on you. If you find that you can handle more, increase your school load by one class each semester. By the time your child graduates from elementary school, you may have your degree—or two!

This may also be a great time to consider working part time if you need to help fatten the family budget or want to save for a Disneyland dream vacation—or better yet, a second honeymoon in Hawaii! I know a group of moms who love working at Starbucks together during the school hours. They have a great time making some extra money. Plus, Starbucks gives full health benefits to part-time employees and offers flexible schedules, making it one of the most mom-friendly companies to work for these days. If you're interested in using your newfound free time to supplement your family income, ask around for mom-friendly places to work in your area.

The options are endless! Take up painting, volunteer to be room mother, or redecorate your house room by room. You may want to purchase a pretty journal and brainstorm a list of "all the things I've wanted to do when I have more time." (Check out your local TJ Maxx or Ross store, if you have one—they have beautiful journals at bargain prices!)

A word to the wise: make sure that you allow yourself a peaceful transition from your world to the world of your children when they come home from school. You need a bit of time to switch gears from "woman at work" (or woman at play!) to mom who is refreshed and ready to give to her kids. Your kids will probably be full of things to talk about, and you need to be ready to listen with interest to the details of their days. They may be famished and in need of a healthy snack, along with a little downtime to rest and perhaps some playtime outdoors. Some moms make their kids tackle their homework right away; others feel that their children need some sort of break, along with fresh air and exercise, before settling down to sit and think. If something has to go in order for your child to be rested and happy, consider having a no-TV rule or limiting TV to one thirty-minute show per day until Friday afternoon.

Even if you are not, by nature, a lover of routine, this is the time to establish traditions, boundaries, and bedtimes for your own sanity and that of your children. The new school schedule may have thrown your child's sleep and eating patterns off-kilter, and he may very well come home emotionally and physically drained. Having weekly meltdowns from information overload isn't uncommon. This is all the more reason to make your after-school routine one that will both relax and energize your children in natural ways. (There's a lot to be said for the old-fashioned after-school routines: debriefing activities of the day, healthy snacks, fresh air and sunshine, rest and play.)

Make a place for your child's homework and paperwork that you need to sign. A small file folder or stacking letter boxes on the kitchen counter often work well—with a different color folder or box for each child.

Miracle Mornings Play by Play

The myth of the miracle morning is that it actually starts in, and only involves, the morning. The true miracle morning starts the evening before and is a continuous, weekly cycle of showering, laying out clothes, loading backpacks, and packing lunches—all before the kids head off to bed. (I have to be honest and admit that after a full school year of packing lunches every day for my charges, we did take advantage of the convenient school lunch program, although each evening we still had to pack a healthy, hearty snack.)

One thing that helps my charges and I have miracle mornings is that we follow a consistent routine, and the kids play a significant role in that routine. This, in turn, has the added benefit of fostering their independence and self-esteem.

Each evening, the kids are responsible for packing their backpacks with schoolwork and other items needed for the next day of classes and laying out their morning clothes on the edge of their beds. Each night, it's the same. They pack their backpacks, shower, lay out clothes, brush their teeth, go to the bathroom, say their prayers, and hit the hay.

When they awake in the morning, they are responsible for getting dressed before they come downstairs and for putting their dirty pajamas in the laundry

> ### *Nanny Tip*
>
> Find a special designated "parking space" for these top five misplaced items so that your miracle-morning routine won't turn into a mess!
> - Backpacks
> - Library books
> - Sporting/practice gear
> - Lunch boxes
> - Homework

bin. They are also responsible for preparing their own breakfast most days, with choices of healthy meals they can easily make themselves: cereal, toast with peanut butter, yogurt with fruit, and so on. They also clean up their own breakfast dishes and do their morning chores—make their beds, brush their teeth, put on their shoes, and place their packed lunches or snacks in their backpacks (which are waiting by the door from the night before!).

When they return home from school, they immediately put their homework folders on the counter, return their backpacks to their "special space" by the door, unpack their lunch boxes, and then are free to play. Although this whole before- and after-school routine takes less than five minutes, it has saved us millions of morning minutes in searching for lost backpacks, folders, or lunch boxes, not to mention aggravation, tears, and hair pulling.

During the day when the kids are at school, I lay out their pajamas so that when five o'clock rolls around, the routine can start again. Eat dinner, pack lunch or snack, pack backpacks, shower, lay out clothes, brush teeth, take a bathroom break, say evening prayers, and then head to bed.

Letting Others Love Your Child

Whenever I think about embarking on a new nanny position, the first thing that crosses my mind is that it is imperative that I work for a mother who refuses to be jealous of the relationship and bond that I form with her children.

I have been fortunate that in my long-term nanny positions, I have never experienced a hint of jealousy from the parents. They unselfishly allow me to love and bond with their children, because they believe it is in the children's best interest. There are no hurt feelings if the kids want to call me in the evening to tell me something or when they chase me out the door to kiss me good-bye—for the third time. They wisely realize that love multiplies; it never divides.

The more people your children learn to love, the more love there is to bounce off the walls of your happy home. It is truly an amazing privilege for a child to have an extra person or two in her life who is willing to play a lasting role in her upbringing. Given our busy lives these days and the increasing number of blended or single-parent families, it really does take a village to raise a child!

All this to say that when your child begins school, she is going to form new relationships with several other adults, including teachers, parents of friends, coaches, and even the lunch lady. The school nurse was a great friend in my charge Austin's life. He bonded with her during his everyday visits to her office, where some ailment would draw him for a pat on the hand or a Band-Aid. I think what he "caught" was the love bug.

Maybe for your child it will be the office lady who greets her with a huge smile every morning or the hockey coach who admires the effort your child puts into the game. Maybe it's even your great-aunt he sees once a year who needs a child to love and spoil! At first, you may have the natural reaction of feeling a twinge of jealousy, since you've been the sole adored adult in your child's life. Fight back this tendency by adopting a "the more, the merrier" approach to your child's bonding.

Stranger Danger

Though we want to encourage our children to enjoy healthy relationships with many adults, we all worry about the possibility of predators taking advantage of our innocent, loving, friendly children. I wish I didn't have to address this issue, but we all know that it's necessary for our children's safety.

There is a fine line that you have to walk, but not cross, when teaching kids about "stranger danger." You have to find the delicate balance of providing enough information to prepare your children for the reality of living in today's world without instilling such fear that they are unable to function in it.

The start of school is a good time to approach the topic of teaching your child to be cautious with some adults, because it's usually the first time your child will be, at times, unsupervised during the day. In preschool, the playgrounds are typically small and fenced in, and your child was likely always accompanied to the bathroom by a trusted adult. In grade school, this usually isn't the case. There are often expansive fields for the children to run and play in, and if they need to go to the restroom, they just take a bathroom pass and head inside the building alone.

I think a good way to begin this delicate discussion is to tell your child that with increasing independence comes increasing responsibility. Your child is now in a place where at times (however brief), he is responsible for himself—and has to learn to be his own protector. The best way to protect ourselves is to know how we

Nanny Tip

Here are some basic safety rules that all parents should teach their child to follow (and be sure to role-play and practice once the rules are laid down):

- Don't talk to people you don't know without asking permission of the adult who is in charge (teacher, parent, etc.).
- Don't take things from anyone (candy, stickers, gifts) without asking permission from the adult who is in charge.
- Don't go with anyone without asking permission from the adult who is in charge.
- Don't give personal information to someone you don't know without permission from the adult who is in charge.
- Never go with anyone who doesn't know the "code word." (Establish a code word that will be used in an emergency if someone other than the normally scheduled person is picking up your child).
- Your body is your body. No one should touch your body without your permission, and if someone does, it should never be a secret. Even in a medical situation, when a doctor must touch your body, it should never be a secret.

can prevent being in an unsafe situation and how to detect one that feels odd and get to safety quickly.

When you warn your child of potential danger from strangers, don't use fear-loaded admonitions like, "Don't take candy from a stranger or you'll be poisoned!" or "Don't get into a car with a stranger or we may never see you again!" These ominous warnings instill nothing but a great sense of fear in the child. They don't empower them to deal with people they don't know or situations they may encounter. Quite often, and sadly, strangers can look like very nice people and may be playing a deceptively kind role in an unwary child's life.

An alternate, more effective approach to educating children about the reality of stranger danger may be instilling the opposite idea in them: that you can't see a person's heart through his or her clothes. You can't tell what type of person someone is by the way he or she looks. So even though nicest-looking people are truly nice, you can't just trust everyone who smiles—especially if they ask you to do something that makes you uncomfortable or you know is wrong.

One very important and simple idea to instill in children is the concept that children are never responsible for adults. Adults help adults. Children do not help adults. Most children fall victim to stranger abductions because they are trying to be helpful, maybe trying to help find a missing dog or a missing child. Tell your child that if an adult asks him for help, he should run inside and get a trusted adult to respond to the "crisis."

Since it is also not uncommon for child abductions or assaults to take place by

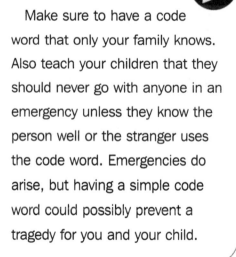

Nanny Tip

Make sure to have a code word that only your family knows. Also teach your children that they should never go with anyone in an emergency unless they know the person well or the stranger uses the code word. Emergencies do arise, but having a simple code word could possibly prevent a tragedy for you and your child.

someone the child knows, all children must be taught to protect themselves from anyone who is not treating them appropriately. This is a lesson that can never be taught too early. Even in my charges' preschool karate class, they were taught about personal respect. They were also taught that their first line of defense is their mouth. If they are in a situation that they are not comfortable with, regardless of who has put them there, they have been taught to say loudly and firmly, "Stop! No! I don't like that!"

Although I have taught my charges over the years that they should respect the adults they know, I have also taught them that if any adult is hurting them, including family or even me, they have permission to say a loud and clear "No!"

If a child is in a situation where she does need help from someone she doesn't know, going to a "safe stranger"—a person of authority in uniform or an adult who is busy (a person working at a store register, a person talking to someone else, or a mom with kids)—is another possible alternative. (Of course, you can also tell them to go to the nearest police officer for help, but realistically, there is a short supply of police officers on the streets today!)

Parents should also teach children the following so that they can get help if they do indeed need it:

- their complete name, address, and phone number;
- how to dial a parent or trusted adult's phone number—from a land line and a cell phone;
- how and when to dial 9-1-1.

Although dealing with strangers is not a fun topic to teach, it is a necessity. The beginning of the school year is always a good time to have a refresher course on stranger safety. The weather is nice, people are out and about, and many children will encounter people whom they do not know, especially if they walk to school.

If you follow the above tips, you will educate and empower your children rather than scare them, so that they can handle with confidence any situation they may face.

Scene 1: Take 2
The First Day of School

MOM, *her voice full of confidence.* Here we go, kiddo. Today's the day!

ZACH, *excitedly.* Yup! I can't wait! *(He walks into school with a spring in his step.)*

MOM, *trying to catch up with her son as he heads toward the school door.* Gimme a hug and kiss!

ZACH. Mom, you don't have to walk me in, you know. I know where my classroom is! *(He Blows a quick kiss in her direction as he greets his friends with a smile.)*

MOM, *sighing.* OK, I see you are getting too old for mushy mom stuff! Wow, you're getting so big and making me so proud. But you owe me a kiss later. Deal? Have a great day, honey. See you at three o'clock.

ZACH. OK! Bye, Mom!

MOM, *turns and exits the school building. Then spying a group of other moms chatting out front, she joins them.* Man, they grow up fast! I never thought the day would come that he wouldn't need me as much. But they all grow up.

SECOND MOM. Yup, sooner or later that time comes for us all, and today just happens to be your day. Let's go grab coffee.

THIRD MOM. I'm game. As long as it's at a place that doesn't use plastic forks or plates or give children's toys in a bag. I'm ready to enjoy a little me time!

Nanny to the Rescue Again!
Recap

How did this mom successfully set up the school day?

1. *She had a positive attitude.* She remained confident and upbeat as she tackled the transition.
2. *She encouraged her child.* She sent him off to school with words of encouragement.
3. *She allowed her child to be independent.* He wanted to walk into class alone, so she respected and supported his decision.
4. *Her mind-set was clear.* She knew that her son's reluctance to be walked into class and kissed good-bye is part of growing up—and she accepted it without taking it personally.
5. *She connected with adults who shared in her experience.* She allowed her experience with her child to connect her with other moms going through the same thing.

CHAPTER TWO

WHERE DID THAT COME FROM?

 Scene 2: Take 1
The Ride Home from School

MOM. How was your day, sweetie?

(Molly shrugs and looks out the window, ignoring the question.)

MOM. Molly, I asked you a question. Did you hear me?

MOLLY. Yeah. Whatever.

MOM. Excuse me?

MOLLY, *oozing sarcasm.* You are excused.

MOM. Whoa. Who are you, and what did you do with my precious, polite little girl?

It may seem like yesterday that your child was struggling to pronounce her first words. But today, you may be wishing she hadn't learned how to speak quite so clearly.

One of the toughest parts of letting your kids go out into the world is the unwanted souvenirs they may bring back home. When you were in charge of most of your child's waking hours, you could monitor her conversations, media choices, and forms of play—and give explanation, correction, or praise when called for. Even though your child's teachers will also be filtering what she sees and hears in the classroom, school days provide plenty of opportunity for other children, who may have been exposed to very different (and sadly, less supervised) home lives, to influence your sweet little girl. Peer pressure seems to be starting earlier and earlier.

No matter the reason for the sudden display of rudeness, how you handle it early on can determine how long it will last.

The Delicate Task of Defusing Your Child's Rudeness Bombs

So what do you do when your child walks out the door in the morning with a positive attitude, full of kindness—and a few hours later, said child (or at least she looks like your child!) returns home with an attitude that is in desperate need of adjustment?

Before you blow up or react . . . take a deep breath. Then tell yourself, "I need to *respond* to this situation rather than *react* to it." Responding involves removing yourself emotionally from what your child has just said (and it isn't easy!) and adopting what I call a "curious bystander" stance.

What, indeed, has transpired in your child's head, or heart, between eight o'clock this morning and three thirty this afternoon? Inquiring parents' minds need to know. But if you react to your child too quickly with anger or shock, she may shut the door to the conversation you really need to have with her—so you can discover what is behind the sudden shift in personality.

It's important that a good conversation, with a positive outcome, happens the first time your child comes home with a " 'tude," because if you just let it go, it is a bit like inviting the Cat in the Hat into your house—easy to let disrespect creep in, hard to get it out. However, for the conversation to be productive, you need to make sure your child is rested, relaxed, and not suffering from the low blood sugar that often hits kids when they are hungry after school (especially with active boys). Low blood sugar, sleepiness, and a stressed-out kid do not make for happy or productive conversations. Many times, the wisest response from you is to postpone a clear-the-air talk until your child is feeling better physically, so you can both handle it with grace and kindness.

More than likely, you are simply the "dog who got kicked" because of a rotten day. Kids tend to lash out at the ones who love them most when they can't have that sort of safety with kids at school. This behavior is not fair to you, and they need to learn better ways to vent, but it is very common. No need to panic when it happens to you, the unsuspecting victim, at some point in your children's school years.

So begin by asking your child, "Do you want to talk right now about what happened to make you answer me rudely, or do you want to go home and get a snack and some rest and then have a chat about it a little later?"

Once you are sure your child is in a good frame of mind (and you are too) and has had a snack and some time to rest or vent alone in her room, begin by saying something that will allow her to be honest, without encouraging more defensiveness. "OK, sugar. I love you, and you know that. In fact, I love you too much to allow you to speak disrespectfully to me the way you did in the car. But because the kind of tone you used is not like the *real* you at all, it tells me something probably happened at school today that hurt your feelings or made you angry. Can you think of anything that happened?"

Allow your child to take her time to open up, without scolding her. Once she has unburdened her heart, and you've done your best to soothe and understand, *then* you can say, "Next time something bad happens and you just don't feel like talking to me right then, you can say, 'Mom, I need a little quiet time now.' I promise I'll let you unwind, rest, and have a snack before we talk about your day. Deal? That way you get a break, and I don't get my feelings hurt by insensitive remarks. There's no need to be rude when we can get what we want with kindness and honesty."

By using this method, you'll preserve the dignity of you and your child, allow for your child to open up when she is ready, and give her practical coping techniques when her little system is simply overloaded. In the Bible, the apostle Paul gave us a wonderful word about balance in conversation with others: "Tell the truth in love."[1] The truth without love can come across as harsh, judgmental, and cruel. However, love without the truth can be coddling and spoiling.

Nanny Tip

Parents tolerate many things, but tolerating any of the following 3Ds can lead to eventual disaster:

1. Disobedience
2. Dishonesty
3. Disrespect

Combat the 3Ds with the 4Cs:

1. *Communicate* your family values.
2. Have *clarity* in your expectations.
3. Be *consistent* in enforcing consequences.
4. Encourage *cooperation* from your children.

Taking the Air out of Peer Pressure

Peer pressure is one of the hardest battles your kids will fight in school. Thinking back to your own childhood, you may remember how strong the push to conform can be. Most of us, under enormous pressure and with immature minds, can remember some point when we gave in to values that didn't line up with our family's beliefs or our own personal code of ethics.

Peer pressure often puts a kid in a position to have to speak against the majority, making your child the minority. He may be stuck in a place where he has to choose whether to make the right decision or the wrong one—and though he might normally choose the right one with ease, he may suffer real embarrassment from his friends by doing so. It's not an easy situation, even for mature adults. However, children who are secure in who they are and have self-worth will be less tempted to fall into peer pressure.

So it is worth taking the time to do all you can to instill in your children a sense of personal worth and power to make the best choices, even if the crowd is leaning the other direction. (Good news for you parents with strong-willed children: when it comes to handling peer pressure, these kids are usually more able to stand against the crowd than compliant children who want to please others at all costs. See? There *is* an upside to every personality type!)

Teaching Self-Worth

There is nothing sweeter than *knowing that you know*, really knowing deep down, that you are loved and appreciated by others. Why? Because it gives you confidence in who you are.

When you are a child, you assess your personal value by the way your family treats you. Your initial internal gauge

> ### Nanny Tip
>
> When asked the question, "Who is your hero?" most children name their parents. In spite of all the peer pressure in the world, you really are the one they look to for their value. If your children know that you value them, they aren't going to care much if others sometimes don't. They will know their worth. They will have seen their value in your eyes.

of self-worth is calibrated by how you are valued by those who say they love you. That's not to say that those who weren't treated ideally as a child will grow up with no sense of self-worth, but it is fair to say that these children will have an uphill climb and may have to work quite hard (by looking to good mentors, reading self-help books, or participating in therapy) to overcome negative thoughts. So how can you teach your child, even during trying times, that he is valued?

Respect your child. By this, I don't mean bow down to his every whim and command. I mean give your child the freedom to express his thoughts and feelings.

Listen to him when he speaks, take the time to hear him out when he feels differently than you do, and give him the benefit of the doubt before you issue judgment. Treat your child as a person, not a possession.

Love your child unconditionally. Always refer to the action that you are unsatisfied with, never the child. Assure her that you love her and that we all make mistakes.

When you mess up, 'fess up. Admit, apologize, and ask for forgiveness when you mess up (since we all do it). It's a priceless life lesson for a child to learn that failure is a part of being human, but forgiving others and ourselves means we can all get fresh starts. What an example to see parents apologize when they are wrong, especially when the child got the wrong end of the stick.

Communicate effectively with your child. Don't just hear her—really *listen* to her words and the tone behind them, and carefully watch her body language to decipher what she is really trying to express. Look her in the eyes when talking with her. One of the rarest and most precious gifts you can give your child is the gift of your rapt attention. The world may not slow down enough to offer this gift; your child is one of twenty or more kids in a busy and crowded classroom. If you and your spouse provide a safe, empathetic place for your child to be heard, it will go a long way in ensuring that your child's sense of self-worth stays intact.

> *Parents need to fill a child's bucket of self-esteem so high that the rest of the world can't poke enough holes to drain it dry.*
> —Alvin Price

Self-Esteem Boosters for Every Day of the Week

Here are a few other ideas to make sure your child knows that what he thinks, says, and does is important to you.

Say more positive than negative things to your child each day. Correct your child, sandwich syle. Start with a positive comment, then insert whatever negative

Nanny Tip

Ten Ways to Praise Your Child

1. Have I told you today what a great kid you are?
2. You're amazing!
3. You're so beautiful—inside and out!
4. Hey there, handsome!
5. You make my heart smile.
6. I am proud of you.
7. You did it! I knew you could!
8. You are one smart cookie!
9. Wow, you are really creative, just like your great-grandmother, the artist!
10. I am glad you are my son/daughter.

comment has to be said. Finally, top off the conversation with another positive slice of affirmation.

Spend some quality one-on-one time with your child each day. Even a quick story (while snuggling if they'll let you in the younger years) sends the message, "You are special and I love you." Shoot some hoops or bake a batch of oatmeal cookies with your grade-school child.

Take pride in your child's accomplishments. Proudly display your child's latest art project, trophy, or school assignment. In fact, check out your local craft store for the wonderful frames that allow you to simply slip your child's latest "van Gogh" in and out of the frame without removing the frame from the wall.

Positively praise your child. Catch her being good, and let her know you notice. "Wow, I really like how organized you are with your schoolwork!"

Give your child responsibilities, and let her reap the rewards. Contributing to the household makes a child feel like part of the team. Setting the table, helping clean up the dishes, making their bed, and putting away their own laundry are all reasonable responsibilities for children that help them feel valued.

Show and tell your child she is loved and valued. Hugs, pats on the back, I love yous, and positive accolades like, "You're my sunshine!" or "Have I told you what a great son you are?" go a long way in promoting self-esteem from the brain to the heart. And although they may claim not to, they secretly still love when you call them by the affectionate nicknames of their younger years.

Be consistent and clear in your expectations so your child can be an achiever. Changing the rules sets up your child for failure. Make your expectations clear to your child, and when she meets them, rejoice together.

Create a Family Code of Honor

For every family, it is important to clearly identify and communicate what I call the family code of honor—a list of the ideals you have for your family. In fact, it

Knights' Code of Honor

- Believe in God and obey His teachings.
- Always obey lawful authorities, as long as they don't conflict with the duties of God.
- Respect and pity the weak, and be steadfast in defending them.
- Love your country.
- Refuse to retreat before the enemy.
- Be courteous to women.
- Be loyal to the truth and the pledged word.
- Be generous in giving.
- Champion the right and the good, in every place and at all times, against the forces of evil.

might be a good idea to tell the story of King Arthur and his knights of the round table and perhaps talk about the knights' code of honor before calling a family meeting to create your own family code. (See sidebar for the knights' code of honor.)

You and your spouse may want to take some time alone to sketch out guidelines that you'd like to have in your family code—all pointing to ways of honoring one another, honoring ourselves, and if you're a family of faith, honoring God. Here are some questions to get you thinking:

> *Respect for ourselves guides our morals, respect for others guides our manners.*
> —Laurence Sterne

- How do you want family members to treat one another?
- What do you believe about God and how to best honor Him with your lives?
- How do you want your family members to treat your home? To treat others?
- What are some practical ways your family can live out your values on a day-to-day basis?
- What sort of toys, media, and language will you allow in the home?
- What expectations do you have of one another outside the walls of your house?

The answers to these questions matter. The greater the sense of legacy and family honor you can build into your children (including how family members treat one another honorably when one member fails or falls short or has a bad day), the greater your child's sense of belonging and self-worth. John Eldredge, author of the best-selling book *Wild at Heart*, says that every man needs a battle to fight, a dragon to slay, and a maiden to rescue.[2] (Sounds like a knight in the making to me!) Instilling in your young boys a sense of a higher destiny and purpose is one of the most important things you can do for them.

Here are some ways to give your children an additional sense of worth and value:

- Volunteer together at a soup kitchen.
- Go on a short-term family mission trip.
- Compliment them when they are kind to kids who feel left out or ignored.
- Teach them how to make others feel warm and appreciated by writing thank-you notes, looking others in the eye and shaking their hand when introduced, using phrases like "Thank you," "May I?" and "Please," and doing small acts of kindness without being asked.
- Always point out the positives and possibilities in every situation. "It is sad that the children were left without their homes in the big flood in New Orleans, but we can help by collecting toys from friends, purchasing toys, sending cards, making them feel welcome in our churches and homes, etc."

Though girls also need to feel called to make a difference in this world, typically they long to be seen as beautiful and appreciated (mind, body, and soul) and to know that God placed in them a uniquely feminine soul with a deep desire to nurture and tenderly care for others.

Whatever you can do to help your children feel they are needed, as lights in this world, with a purpose to accomplish—do it! In parenting, as in life, it is better to light a candle than shout at the darkness. If you put your efforts into giving your children a sense of value, worth, and contribution to the world, you will automatically lessen the amount of time you'll spend "shouting at the darkness"— like saying no to watching questionable movies, listening to music with lyrics that dishonor women, or wasting time in front of the TV or video games.

Remember, your family code applies to the entire family, not just the kids. When you make your family code, be sure to only include the things that you are willing and ready to consistently enforce—and be sure to have a consequence ready for breaking the family code, such as time-outs or loss of privileges. It's one for all and all for one!

Respect the Code of Others Without Breaking Your Own

Now that your children know that your family has its own code of honor, what should they do when confronted by others who have a completely different moral code?

Begin by being honest with your child. Explain that the way your family does things isn't necessarily the way that other families do things, nor does it mean that your way is always right. Teach your children that they've been raised by the standards you feel are best, from your years of experience and wisdom. Clearly communicate that your family's code of honor is the way things will be done in your home . . . without placing harsh judgment on others who choose to live their lives differently. And if your children balk at your rules, remind them that someday they will be adults and can establish their own code of honor for themselves and their family.

There is no avoiding this sad reality: kids will get teased, and often it is because of their beliefs. Maybe your child will be labeled a "goody-goody" because he refuses to participate in trash talk. Perhaps your child will be labeled the "teacher's pet" because she respects her adult authority. Prepare your kids for these potential scenarios, and reassure them that nearly all of the great men and women who have stood up for right in the face of wrong have been ridiculed or teased. In fact, one of the best things you can do with your children is to read them biographies of great men and women who stood up for good causes in the face of opposition. There are many books on various reading levels that tell the stories of men and women of integrity who bravely stood up for their beliefs, such as Harriet Tubman, Abraham Lincoln, Martin Luther King Jr., Rosa Parks, Mother Teresa, and others.

A word of caution and encouragement: even if you were to do everything perfectly, your kids are human, and at one time or another they are probably going to

> ### Nanny Tip
>
> Encourage your children to be leaders by allowing them to make some of their own decisions. (You know, those choices you know *you* really want to make but know your child is completely able to make on his own?)
>
> Next time your child wants to pick out his own outfit, choose her own hairstyle, or rearrange his room, suppress the automatic urge to dictate your preferences. It builds self-esteem for a child to have control over some of his own life choices, especially in areas that aren't vitally important to his long-term well-being.

give in to their peers and do or say something that is less than ideal. This is part of growing up. With your loving guidance, they'll get back on track—hopefully with a valuable lesson tucked into their maturing hearts.

Be the Leader, Not the Follower

Remember the television show *Happy Days*? The Fonz could simply walk into a room and snap his fingers, and teens would line up to do his bidding. (Sometimes he'd hit the wall with the side of his fist and the lights would dim. Even the electricity cooperated with Fonzie's irresistible aura! How'd he *do* that?) Then there was Richie Cunningham, who was typically more of a follower.

In this world, there seem to be Fonzies and Richies—leaders and followers—and kids recognize the difference by sheer instinct. But if you watch *Happy Days* through its seasons of growth, you observe Richie being mentored by a loving mom and dad. Before long, the day comes when he becomes a leader in his own right. You may have a child like Richie, who has started out as more of a follower. But with wonderful mentors and God's help, your child may enjoy amazing experiences in leadership someday. (He probably won't be able to make the lights dim by hitting the wall with his fist, however.)

Although some will say that kids who lead and kids who follow are determined by pure personality, I believe that you have great influence in helping your children be the ones who set the standard rather than follow the herd. Leaders grow up from children who have found their self-confidence early. They tend to come from homes where they weren't given mixed signals and where their parents or caregivers had high expectations for their behavior.

The standards in the homes where I nanny aren't wishy-washy. By age six, my charges would tell me that they didn't want to have a playdate with certain children because their behavior was rude or mean. At their young age, they were already forming an internal monitor of acceptable and unacceptable behavior, and I couldn't have been more proud.

Kids Can Be Role Models Too

I always encourage kids to be role models. It empowers them and builds self-confidence when they feel that their behavior choices are so important that they can affect others.

When a classmate was in a bad-behavior rut, one of my charges would say on the way to school, "Today I am going to sit next to Jimmy and do extra-good behavior so that he wants to do it too!" When observing a kid throwing a fit in a restaurant or whining for candy at the grocery store, they would often tell me, "Shell, we don't want *that* to rub off on us." I couldn't help but giggle, but I was inwardly glowing—pleased that they were observing behaviors around them and making great choices.

> *Be a yardstick of quality. Some people aren't used to an environment where excellence is expected.*
> —Stephen Jobs

Here are a few more points to keep in mind when building up your child's sense of internal value so they can withstand the winds of peer pressure.

Avoid labeling a child. Labels are often like a self-fulfilling prophecy. If you speak it, they will live up to it. Labeling affects the way a child sees himself, the way others see him, and the way others treat him.

Address the behavior, not the child. All children are great gifts from God. They are good—although at times their behavior stinks. (If it seems that I'm repeating this point over and over again, I plead guilty. I know how easy it is to start thinking of a child as the bad seed when he is strong-willed or has ADD or gets on your last nerve. By mentally removing a child's temporarily bad behavior from his true and best self, you'll be a much better parent—and none of your children will grow up with the black sheep label hanging over their heads.)

Be a cheerleader. Positive, purposeful praise goes a long way. "I really like the way you helped to clear the table. Thanks for pitching in without my even asking you to!" Praise like this says to your child, "Your effort was recognized, appreciated, and valued. You made a difference."

Give your child the gift of your time. Taking a few minutes each day to give your child your undivided attention will have a lasting impact on how she feels about herself.

Teach your child to accept all people for who they are. Have the mind-set that all people are different and that different doesn't always mean right or wrong. There's a fine line between holding to your family code and looking down on others who choose differently. Affirm that everyone has worth; all people are loved by God, even if we don't always agree. Talk to your children about patience, forgiveness, and tolerance with people who are struggling and perhaps going in a wrong path. Teach them to guard their boundaries against the school bully, but also help them to say a prayer for the bully's hurting heart and understand that a child's mean behavior may come from a very sad home life. It is good to teach your child early that "hurting people hurt people."

Set reasonable limits. Children want to please their parents. How can they do that if they don't understand the expectations that you have set for them? Set realistic limits for your children. If your kids have no demands on them, they have no chance to prove themselves. But if your demands are unrealistic, your children will be set up for constant failure.

Treat your child as a person, not a possession. Give your children eye contact when communicating, avoid embarrassing them in front of their peers, and allow them to express themselves (respectfully) to you.

Building your child's self-confidence will make her a self-assured individual, with deep roots of confidence that can withstand the hurricanes of pressure, temptation, and opposition. She'll be comfortable with who she is, and she'll be comfortable with letting the world know it!

Scene 2: Take 2
The Ride Home from School

MOM. How was your day, sweetie?

Molly shrugs and looks out the window, ignoring the question.

MOM. Molly, I asked you a question. Did you hear me?

MOLLY. Yeah. Whatever.

MOM. Excuse me?

MOLLY, *oozing sarcasm.* You are excused.

MOM, *taking a deep breath and praying for wisdom about how to handle this sudden and rude behavior with truth and love.* Molly, this kind of disrespect isn't like you. We need to talk about this, but I want to do it when you are feeling up to it. If you are hungry or tired, let's wait until we get home. But before suppertime, I'd like to know what made you say such hurtful words to me—when you are able to tell me, respectfully and kindly.

MOLLY, *tears filling her eyes*. Mom, everyone thinks I'm teacher's pet because I'm so nice, and kids are teasing me.

MOM. Well, sweetie, that must have really hurt your feelings. Did it make you feel better to be rude to me? Do you feel any "cooler" now?

MOLLY. No, it feels awful.

MOM. Well, hon, it seems like your heart is telling you the truth. Regardless of what others say, you need to be *you*. You are kind and thoughtful and respectful to adults, and it makes you feel warm and happy inside to be that way.

MOLLY. Yeah, but what do I tell the kids?

MOM, *thinking*. Hmm . . . How about, "I like being me. And I'm going to keep being me. I'm kind and funny and respectful, and I think that's a great thing"?

MOLLY, *grinning*. You forgot some things.

MOM. What's that?

MOLLY. I'm really pretty, and I'm the best three-point shooter in basketball . . . and, and . . . I'm very humble.

MOM, *laughing*. That's my girl! Welcome back!

 ## Nanny to the Rescue Again! Recap

How did this mom turn her child's terrible behavior into a terrific teaching moment?

1. *She addressed the behavior, not the child.*
2. *She gave her child the benefit of the doubt.* She realized this wasn't her daughter's usual behavior and concluded that something must have been behind it.

3. *She gave her child an opportunity to get herself together.* She offered to postpone the conversation and gave her daughter the option to eat something, rest, or have a bit of space to think about what just occurred.

4. *She listened to and validated her child's feelings.* She acknowledged that it is no fun to be teased and that it is hard to make the right choices.

5. *She praised her child for making a good choice.*

6. *She reassured her child that it was OK to be herself.* She reminded her daughter that feeling good about your choices and yourself is what counts.

CHAPTER THREE

WHY CAN'T I?
HER MOTHER LETS HER DO IT!

 ### Scene 3: Take 1
In the Family Room

TOMMY. Mom, can I get the new Fifty Cent CD?

MOM. No, you can't.

TOMMY. But why not? Jake's mom let him get it.

MOM. Well, I'm not Jake's mom.

TOMMY. Mom, come on. Everyone has it. Fifty Cent rocks.

MOM. No. Ask me again, and you're gonna see Mom rock her way into your room to disconnect your CD player.

TOMMY. But, Mom . . .

MOM, *irritated.* No! You aren't getting it, and that's final.

A h, the good old days. In the toddler years things were noisy, for sure, but the basic plan was simple: Mom said yes; child said no. Mom responded with a firm yes, took the child by the hand, and off they went to bed . . . or away from the candy machine . . . or from the playground to the car and home for a nap. Easy, straightforward, simple. No confusion, and no room for mixed messages. You said yes because you wanted obedience to your request. Your child said no because . . . well, mostly because she loved hearing herself say such a powerful word! Because a two-year-old has not entered into the age of reasoning, you didn't waste your limited parental energy trying to reason with her, using logic she couldn't begin to grasp. (If you did, you obviously didn't read my first book!)

Thankfully, your child has now grown out of the "world totally revolves around me" mentality and has now begun the "world should revolve around me but sadly does not" mentality. He is well on his way to grasping the fine skills of negotiating and reasoning, accepting what is realistic in a world filled with ups and downs and other people's feelings.

In this new era, Mom says no and child says, "But . . ." Yes, this stage of child development is known as "The Age of Buts" in my personal nanny research files. Buts in the morning. Buts at noontime. Buts when the sun goes down.

"No, you can't."

"*But* Sarah can! . . . *But* it seems safe! . . . *But* it looks fun! . . . *But* everyone else is doing it!"

Who doesn't remember their mother asking, "If Mary jumped off a bridge, would you do it?" I wonder if this clichéd line of questioning started in the Stone Age. I can just imagine some cave mom lecturing, "If Thor jumped off a cliff, would you do it?" I can just as easily imagine an active, headstrong, nine-year-old cave son pausing to consider the possibility for a moment, weighing the fun-versus-pain factor.

This is the age where kids love using their own minds, which in the long run is great! We want them to become independent thinkers. It's just that a fifth-grade boy's mind is not exactly somewhere you'd want to go into alone quite yet. Their thinking is intact; but wisdom is intelligence mixed with life experience, and they are still awfully short on experience. The goal, then, is to foster your child's newfound ability to reason but help guide him with your hard-earned years of experience. It's not easy, for school years are a time of peer pressure and outside influence. You may still be their true number one hero, but that doesn't mean you don't have some stiff competition out there!

Social Changes from First Through Sixth Grade

Between first grade and sixth grade, ages six-ish to twelve-ish, your child will undergo many social changes. Here is a brief grade-by-grade breakdown adapted from www.familyeducation.com to help you get a grasp on your child's level of reasoning ability.

First grade. Kids tend to want to be the best; they want to be first. They have tons of energy and are just learning to distinguish between fantasy and reality. It is also a time when children begin to discover who they are.

Second grade. Kids really begin to grasp reasoning and concrete thinking. They begin to worry and can be critical about themselves. They often despise being singled out among their peers and having the focus on them.

Third grade. Kids enter the know-it-all stage. At this age, children will often set unrealistic goals for themselves because they are eager to know and discover what the world has to offer. During this time of discovery, they will quickly begin to comprehend that every action has an equal and opposite reaction—that even their own personal choices and actions have consequences.

Fourth grade. The year of rebellion, the year of seeking independence at all costs. Being part of the group can become more important than doing what is right. Their emotions are in full swing, and they are learning to clearly express them. Their confidence may be lacking, but you may not be able to see through the front.

Fifth grade. A positive attitude is reborn. Truthfulness, obedience, self-confidence, maturity, and good communication skills are qualities that are entering full bloom.

Kids begin to accept others, even those who are different. Strong friendships are being built. It is also a time where a need for multimedia enters the picture: TV, videos, games, MP3s, and the computer take top priority.

Sixth grade. Children begin to be assertive and express their wide range of feelings quite well. The competitive spirit strongly emerges, which can manifest itself in negative behavior, including putting down peers, teasing classmates, and making inappropriate jokes and comments.

This is a general overview, but by no means is it a complete or concrete definition of all kids at these ages and stages. Their personalities will also determine how your children act at each grade level.

Testing Your Authority

Grade-school children begin to question the authority not only of their parents but also of teachers and other adult leaders. They've seen that adults can make mistakes, too, so they no longer give any adult absolute, all-powerful authority. Which is a good thing. You don't want your child to trust and obey *every* adult. There are some untrustworthy grown-ups out there, as we all know too well. So don't be too upset by your children's natural tendency to question authority; it has some value.

As your kids begin to reason and make decisions for themselves, they may naturally begin to wonder if your way is truly best—and ponder what would happen if they tried a different route. They will test you. This testing can come in many forms.

The Passive-Aggressive Approach

The subtlest form of a child's questioning of your authority is ignoring you, reinterpreting your commands as suggestions, or perhaps changing your words to say what they want you to say. "Oh, I didn't hear you." Or, "I thought you meant to take the trash out of the can and put it on the kitchen table. You didn't say to take the trash *out to the curb.*" Or, "Oh, I thought you said to *mess up* my room. Did you mean I was supposed to clean it?" Then there's just the plain old lack of acknowledgment of what just left your lips. The silent response. Or maybe a grumbled, "Huh?"

Of course, there will be times where your child will just be so enthralled with what she is doing that she genuinely didn't hear you. However, if this isn't the case, most likely the ignoring is really her way of saying, "I really don't like that request."

In times like this, before you blow, quickly evaluate the situation with three questions:

1. Was your request or rule clear?
2. Was your request or rule simple enough for your child to comprehend and execute?
3. Have you been following through on enforcing the request or rule?

Nanny Tip

Make sure you only offer your children the two choices you are prepared to live with.

If the answer is yes to all of the above, then your child's behavior may be an issue of perceived control. Whether it makes sense to you or not, your child may be feeling smothered and ordered around. An effective way of addressing this reaction is to empower a child by giving her choices that you can live with. "We are leaving now. Shut the TV off, or I will shut it off." "You can't play ball in the house, but you can play outside." And my personal favorite, "You can watch PBS Kids or nothing." Kids seem to listen more readily when you offer two choices, because they have to think through the alternatives. Fairly quickly, their ears will miraculously reopen and they will respond to you.

If you end the request with a question, they have to engage even more, and you get the satisfaction of making sure they both heard and comprehended you. For example, try saying, "You can read for a half hour or watch thirty minutes of TV before bedtime. Which would you rather do?" When they say, "Watch TV for thirty minutes," they've been empowered by making a choice, within boundaries, and you know they both heard you and comprehended you.

Outright Defiance

Then there are occasions when your child shows outright defiance. This is when, in essence, he declares, "No. I am not going to do it, and you can't make me."

This is where consistency pays off. "Leave no line blurred" is my philosophy in dealing with children from infancy to adulthood, especially when it comes to the basics of respect and the consequences of reacting to their parents without it. Children should feel safe enough to share their realistic thoughts and concerns or alternative viewpoints with you, but they need to be taught (and reinforced) how to challenge without being rude and disrespectful.

For example, if a fourth grader said to me, "No, I won't do that. You are a jerk, and I hate you!" I would say to the child (after counting silently to ten), "You know the consequences for rude responses to me. Would you like to restate that response before we continue our discussion in a way that is more honoring?" Give them one chance to state their feelings in a kinder and gentler way. If they do not, the behavior must have consistent consequences. For example, in the families for whom I nanny, rude behavior always results in an apology and a time-out.

To Ground or Not to Ground

Though many parents use grounding as a method to teach their kids respect and obedience, I have never really seen much benefit to it. I prefer giving the kid something constructive to do, preferably something he really doesn't like. This way it is a win-win. Your child is too busy to do much introspective brooding, he's feeling some productive pain, and you may get the weeds pulled from your garden. Another positive aspect of putting your kid to work to pay off his disobedience debt is that you can often create a one-to-one, logical correlation between the offense and the correction. Research has proven that the more you can tie the offense to the consequence, the better a child understands.

Here are a couple of examples. John talks back to you in a disrespectful tone when you've made a perfectly logical and kind request. His discipline might be to do the request plus an additional chore, then write "Ten Ways I Could Have Responded to Mom in a More Honoring Way." You've tied his knee-jerk offense in with a thoughtful, proactive, and positive redirecting of his thoughts. Learning how he could have done this differently is a key component of recovering from mistakes.

Conflict is inevitable, but combat is optional.
—Max Lucado

Another example: You asked Maria to clean her room and she "forgot"—two days in a row. You have Maria sit down at the kitchen table and write out a chart for herself on how she will clean her room today—exactly where she will begin and what she will do and how much time she thinks it will take. (For example: "Pick up clothes from floor—five minutes. Make bed—one minute.") Then have her write a list of three ways she can keep her room clean on a daily basis. ("I'll hang up my school clothes before going outside to play. I'll make my bed first thing in the morning." And so forth.)

It takes a bit of thinking on your part, Mom and Dad. But the long-term benefits are worth the time it takes to come up with logical consequences that somehow connect the correction to the offense.

Compromise

Thankfully, your children are at an age where you can compromise with them in the sort of respectful, give-and-take way that adults employ in mature relationships. For example, "I understand that you enjoy painting, but it makes a huge mess. How about we compromise? You cover the table with newspaper first and clean up the mess afterward, and you can paint to your heart's content. Deal?" Or, "Sure, you can play football, but it needs to be outside."

Small ways of valuing and respecting your child will help her self-worth. "I understand that you would prefer to go with Stacie, but we already have plans with Grandma today. Let's look at the calendar right now and plan a fun day out with Stacie. What would you like to do with her, and when would be a good afternoon for an outing?"

Choose Your Battles

If you are struggling with a defiant child, try to choose your battles. Your preference for him to wear matching socks to school may need to take a backseat to his using inappropriate language. Choose your battles around what matters most. It is always wiser to emphasize character over outward appearances. Emphasize how to heal, redirect, and train a child to be kinder, more thoughtful, more cheerful—rather than how he is wearing his hair today or his choice of clothes. When he asks you, "Why do I have to clean my room?" rather than responding, "Because I like a clean house, and your room embarrasses me," try saying, "Because how you keep your room is a message about how you value yourself. You deserve a space that is clean, ordered, and beautiful to live in, don't you think?"

Now back to the kind of questions that started this chapter: "Why can Olivia watch a PG-13-rated movie but I can't?" "Why can Scotty attend sleepovers but I can't?" "Why does Lisa's mom let her ride in the back without a seat belt and I have to wear one?" "Why is your way different? It's not fair!" "But he can! . . . But she can!" How's a parent to respond?

Set Clear Standards in Your Family Code

As previously mentioned, your family code consists of what is and isn't acceptable in your family. It includes the behaviors and activities that you, as a family, approve of. It is the standard that you all, together, have set for your family. Whether you write it out on paper and discuss it as a family, or acknowledge it with your words and actions, your family code should be mutually established.

If your child has started protesting, "But he can . . . why can't I?" now may be a good time to revisit the family code, which is written in generalities. By looking at the code, decide some concrete family rules that you can keep on a regular basis.

Here are some questions to get you started: What types of TV shows are your children allowed to watch? What kind of language is permitted in your home? Which behaviors are deemed acceptable, and which are unacceptable? What types of toys are your children allowed to play with? What styles of clothing are your kids allowed to wear? What kinds of boundaries and limits are enforced? Do your children play unsupervised or supervised when friends are over? Do they have unlimited access to the computer or Internet? Are they allowed to take their Game Boy to school? Do you expect good grades? Do you encourage your children to finish what they start? Do you attend church? Do you require the kids to take part in charitable activities?

The answers to these specific questions can be found by referring back to the general rules of your family's code. It should be, to your children, like the "knights' code of honor"—reverenced and accepted. All for one and one for all.

So when your ten-year-old asks why he can't see a PG-13 movie, you can say, "Because I've looked it up online, and there are scenes in that movie that aren't honoring to women. There is language that turns God's name into a cuss word. Our family code states, 'We honor God and others in all we watch, say, and do.' This means, for now, we choose to watch a different sort of movie. When you are older, you can make your own code or adjust our family code. But for now, it is what it is."

It may be tempting to give in to their whines of "Joshua's mother lets him play cop-killing video games" or "Sarah got to see that R-rated movie!" But if you give in once, you've opened Pandora's box to more. Better to have set rules in your family code of honor and to be firm with enforcing them every time you are tested.

What you allow your children to hear or see gives the impression to your child that you are OK with what they are hearing or seeing. In today's culture, this often means you are opening the door that has the ability to knock your kid on the head and leave a permanent bump. It probably goes without saying that fil-

Sample Family Code of Honor

In our family, we do the following:

- Value each other as part of a team.
- Obey our parents.
- Use our words, not our hands.
- Build one another up, never tear others down.
- Refrain from swearing and using other inappropriate language.
- Respect others. We treat others as we want to be treated.
- Do our best, always trying our hardest and finishing what we start.
- Keep our word. We mean what we say and say what we mean.
- Always tell the truth.
- Help others by giving back to the community.
- Respect ourselves and keep our bodies and minds healthy (exercise; eat nutritional meals; don't smoke, drink, or use drugs; watch family-approved TV shows and movies; visit family-approved Web sites; and listen to family-approved music).

And if you are a family of faith, you may wish to include these:

- Regularly serve in our local church.
- Honor God and others in all we watch, say, and do.

ters on the computer or satellite TV, and even a good monitoring of the magazines and books that come into your home, are essential. Kids are bombarded

today by so much more than they
have the ability to handle. Lovingly
set limits that will protect their
minds and hearts.

It is also important to acknowledge that not all families have the
same code. Some families may allow
a child to stay home alone and unsupervised at age ten; others will wait
until age thirteen. Some families
have no objections to their children
watching R-rated movies when a
parent is with them; some do. Some
families believe in God; others don't.
It is important to share with your
child that although different families
have different rules and expectations, the ones that you have set for
your family are the ones that you
believe work best, based on your life
experience and your religious beliefs.

As we mentioned in the previous
chapter, you need to express the
importance of your family code with-

Nanny Tip

When you find yourself
talking in circles with your child
about why he can't do something,
it never hurts to give a generic,
stock answer that ends the
conversation. Something like, "It's
just not something our family does"
with a brief explanation of why. Or,
"That's just the way it is. Though I
understand you don't agree, your
dad and I are the bosses of the
house. When you are a parent
someday, you get to be the boss!"
Or, "You can't go to the movies
alone, because it's not something
that happens in our family until a
child turns thirteen." These
lessons reaffirm your family's
code of honor.

out judging the code of another. Convey to your children that when others are in
your home, they are expected to follow your rules—but assure your child that if
needed, you don't mind being the "bad guy" and explaining the rules (nicely) to
their friends and enforcing them.

I remember that when my best friend was in about fifth grade, she wasn't allowed to watch movies unless they were first approved by her parents. At a friend's house one day, she watched an unapproved movie. Her conscience began to bother her about halfway through the video, and she called her parents to come get her. She was upset with herself because she had betrayed her family code and her parents' trust. Her parents reassured her of their trust and applauded the courage it took for her to make that phone call. In fact, they promised never to scold her anytime she found herself in a bad situation as a result of a bad choice and called them for help.

You may be deceived if you trust too much, but you will live in torment if you don't trust enough.
—Frank Crane

When your child becomes a teen and has a first drink at a party—a result of peer pressure perhaps, or just curiosity—and finds he is too intoxicated to drive home, you want to have established such a home of grace and acceptance that your teen will have no fear of calling you, explaining the situation, and asking for your help. How many teens killed by driving home drunk could have been saved if they felt safe enough to call Mom or Dad to pick them up, with no lectures?

A Family Code Your Kids Will Respect

If you want your kids to respect your family code, do the following:

Clearly define your code. Your family code should include your house rules, your behavioral exceptions, and what you do and do not approve of in activities and entertainment.

Consider what you are willing to enforce. Only include what you are ready to regularly monitor in your code. A code without a penalty for breaking it is meaningless.

Consistently enforce the code. Do not allow for exceptions, unless you give a clear explanation. As kids grow older and mature, you can make more exceptions to your code because they can understand the reasoning behind your change of mind.

Create concrete consequences. Carefully plan disciplinary action for breaking the code. Time-out, losing a privilege, having a toy taken away—whatever it is, be up front with your kids about the consequences of breaking the code.

Constantly monitor your emotions. Be calm but firm when redirecting your child. Also, be honest—speak the truth in love. An example in my life as a nanny was when my first-grade charge drew a comic with a word balloon saying, "I'm gonna kill you!" *Hmm. How precious.* I took a moment to think how to respond and said, "Austin, this is a really fabulous drawing, but I am disappointed that you chose to use 'kill' in your comic, because killing someone isn't funny. Let's think of something else we could have written with this wonderful piece of artwork." He responded, "Shell, I knew you were going to say that. I was copying my library book, and you are right. I could have said, 'Watch out! I am going to get you!' That would have been more appropriate." (Yes, I know it sounds funny, but Austin really used those exact words. Both of my charges learned the phrase *appropriate behavior* by the time they were eighteen months old!)

You may be in a period of parenting where you feel like your children are testing you all the time. Let me reassure you that what they really want and need, no matter what they are saying, is to hear you come back with consistent answers that affirm your family code. Though they may be begging to go to a party where there will be no parents on a school night, what they want to hear is, "You know the rules, buddy. And they aren't going to bend. I'm giving you the gift of safety and security and trust in our consistency, even though you are testing me."

As kids get older, time continues to build up trust, so you can begin to compromise and give your child opportunities to make his own decisions. When he is thirteen, you and he can revisit the subject of PG-13 movies and perhaps make some compromises on certain films once you've both read the reviews.

Nanny Tip

Not only does your child need to earn your trust, but you also need to earn the trust of your child. Here are some ways to build trust with your child:

- Listen to your child without being overly emotional about what she says.
- Help your child find the right answers by walking him through the decision-making process and teaching him to weigh the pros and cons of situations.
- Model trustworthiness by making good decisions, being consistent, and telling the truth.
- Meet your child's physical and emotional needs daily.
- Teach your child the "no secret between kids and parents" rule. If something is bothering him or doesn't feel right, encourage him to share it with you.
- Give your child permission to say no to things that don't make him feel safe. For example, if a friend is encouraging him to take part in an inappropriate activity, like throwing rocks at a classmate, remind him it's OK to say no.
- Give your child private time where she can make her own decisions in a safe environment. Let her have time in her bedroom alone. Check in occasionally, but give her the opportunity to be on her own.
- Give your child opportunities to build your trust by giving him responsibilities and bits of freedom where he has a chance to make a choice.

Trust Training

According to *Webster's Dictionary*, trust is the "firm reliance on the integrity, ability, or character of a person." It's having confidence that your child will make the right decision, and it is built over time.

How do you build trust? By giving opportunities for your child to earn it. A child always receives your love for free, but trust must be earned and privileges must be granted for each test passed. When your child has a choice and makes the "right" decision, the one that lines up with your family code, he earns your trust. Make it clear each time you give your child a new freedom that this freedom is a test. If he honors his new freedom, he'll get more privileges. If he proves that he can't handle the freedom, you'll have to remove privileges.

Here are some ways to implement trust training with your child.

Leave your child in a room and ask him to wait there for a minute. Finding him when you return is passing the test of trust.

Praise honesty. Notice when your child is honest, and praise him for it. When he doesn't lie even when he could have, reward that with positive praise or a small token showing that you are proud he made the right decision.

Praise responsibility. When your child makes a good judgment, fulfills an obligation, or demonstrates behavior that goes above and beyond the expected, reward him.

Give your child some freedom and opportunity to make his own choices. For example, bring him to the video store and ask him to select a movie. Does he make an appropriate choice? If so, he's passed a test and maybe the reward can be a little unmonitored TV time.

Of course, your child isn't going to pass every test. There will be trial and error, two steps forward and one step back. When your child does fail, impose a consequence. After the disciplinary action has been fulfilled, give him new opportunities to prove himself—little by little.

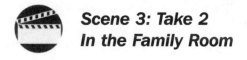

Scene 3: Take 2
In the Family Room

TOMMY. Mom, can I get the new Fifty Cent CD?

MOM. No, honey, you can't.

TOMMY. But why not? Jake's mom got it for him.

MOM. Well, I'm not Jake's mom, and we don't live by Jake's family rules. Listen, Tommy, I understand how it feels not to have the "in" thing, but we can't always have what everyone else has. I don't approve of the language this musician uses, and I don't think you need to listen to negative music that talks about violence. Listening to that type of music goes against the family code, and in your heart, I think you know that.

TOMMY. But, Mom . . .

MOM. Tommy, think about it. Am I saying no because I want to be mean? Or am I saying no because I love you and care about what goes in your ears to your brain?

TOMMY, *sighing*. Because you love me.

MOM. You got *that* right. Let's look at some other artists who might have the same sound you like, but have better words.

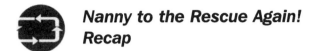

Nanny to the Rescue Again!
Recap

How did this mom put an end to the musical mayhem?

1. *She listened to her child and validated his feelings.* "You're right. It's no fun not having what everyone else has."
2. *She was calm but firm.* She didn't lose her temper, but she didn't compromise her family code either.
3. *She sent a clear signal.* Her decision wasn't wishy-washy. The family code was clear, and the CD violated that code, so she didn't have to wonder whether she was making the right decision.
4. *She enforced her family's code.* Violence was not part of the code, so music that talks about violence wasn't allowed.
5. *She avoided putting down his friend's mom.* She explained that different families have different rules.
6. *She gave him the reason behind her response.* "I care about you; that is why the answer is no."
7. *She gave him a positive alternative.* She offered to help him find another CD with a similar sound and feel, but with lyrics that wouldn't contradict their family code.

SECTION TWO

SCHOOL DAYS, PLAY DAYS

CHAPTER FOUR

THE GREAT SCHOOL DEBATE

 ### Scene 4: Take 1
Sitting at Starbucks

MARY, *to the Monday Moms Coffee Club*. So it's almost March 10, and you
know what that means: we'll know if Lucy got into private school.

KATRINA. Well, if you ask me, the public schools here are just fine. They are
what you make of them, and if you stay involved and on top of things,
the kids do just as well.

PATRICIA, *sighing*. Well, ladies, I'm glad I don't have to worry about that. The
charter-school planning has been going so well. It's like a private public
school—all the perks and none of the payments. We signed up, and I
can't wait to see how Katie does.

KATRINA. Mary, how many schools did you apply to, and what made you
choose them?

MARY, *with an air of superiority*. We have the backup private school, the decent
private school, and the ultimate private school. But really, as long as we
get into one of them, I'm sure Lucy is on the straightest track to
Harvard. There really is no possibility that a child can get the sort of
high-level education she needs outside of a good, expensive private
school—if she wants to go to an Ivy League university, that is. Of
course, not all children aspire to such heights.

As a high school sophomore in a public school, I decided that I wanted to attend Simmons College, an all-women's private, prestigious university in Boston. It was the only school I wanted to apply to. My guidance counselor suggested I create a backup plan, but I refused. I even applied early, declaring a major in the most competitive field at the time: physical therapy. I was one of fifty candidates who got accepted and received a huge financial aid package that covered the cost of the hefty tuition. I was thrilled to be attending.

Once I got there, I lasted just two months. I didn't feel at home—and it wasn't just the discomfort of the dorm bed. I had grown up in a rural middle-class suburb and was transplanted in what seemed like the culture capital of the world. I felt like an elephant in a city. All of a sudden, my comforts of home were replaced with unfamiliar surroundings, circumstances, and people. The huge flood of diverse cultures, political and religious viewpoints, and personalities overwhelmed me at that time in my young life. I could barely concentrate on my schoolwork with what amounted to too much stimuli and freedom for my Container Store personality type.

I have never let my schooling interfere with my education.
—Mark Twain

To my own surprise, I found I liked the sheltered life I lived, and I wanted it back! Some kids thrive on their newfound freedom when they leave home; I happenned to be one of those homebodies who preferred taking college courses near the familiarity of home and hearth.

Where one young woman might have thrived in the excitement and bustle of the city, this country mouse was in continuous culture shock, experiencing too much change at once for me to concentrate well on my schoolwork. So I withdrew from the school (do you know they make you see a psychologist before they allow you to do that?) and worked as a nanny for the remainder of that semester.

When November came around, I walked onto the local campus of my state university, Bridgewater State College. I told the admissions officer that I had left

Simmons and wanted to enroll at their school for the fall semester. With raised eyebrows, the officer directed me immediately to her superior, the admissions director. She, too, looked at me as if I'd suddenly sprouted daisies from the top of my head. I'll never forget what she said: "Why would you ever want to come here if you could go there? That is a ridiculous decision." In fact, she thought it was so ridiculous that the admissions board was hesitant to allow me in!

Once I was accepted, it actually cost me more out-of-my-own-pocket money to attend a state school than it did a prestigious university. Yet I thrived in this homey, rural atmosphere where you might have to dodge a cow or two crossing a pasture but never worry about a speeding motorist on a busy street. Though there was definitely diversity in my small town, for me it was on a much more manageable scale. I also lived at home and commuted to class, discovering there ain't nothing like your own bed and Mama's cooking to keep your spirits—and grades—up.

> ### Nanny Tip
>
> Regardless of which avenue of education you choose for your child, you can give your child the two gifts my mother gave me to help ensure my success:
>
> 1. Do all you can to match your child's personality and needs to an educational environment in which she will bloom, regardless of status or prestige.
> 2. Help her get enthused about opportunities to learn about the world she lives in, and encourage her curiosity and enjoyment of academic challenges by taking full advantage of her education.

So what's the point? Education is not a one-school-fits-all proposition. Even though it seemed illogical for me to go against the prestigious flow, I performed better where I was comfortable. I succeeded when I felt secure.

Not only did my mother understand and encourage me to bloom where I felt nourished as a student (regardless of the prestige factor), but she also instilled in me the value of taking advantage of every educational opportunity whenever and wherever it was available. As a result, during my senior year of high school, I took the tough classes instead of taking electives or leaving early for work-study programs. I took advantage of all that was available to me in high school, where college-level courses were free and I could better prepare for university experiences.

I am not here to advise you on which type of education is best for your child but rather to point out the pros and cons of the three major choices: public, private, and homeschooled education. Charter schools have provided a fourth choice that has worked beautifully for many families.

Although there are pros and cons to each educational option, what really is important is that you pick the best educational route for your child. What type of learning environment would best suit his needs? What can provide him with the best opportunity to excel? What school philosophy lines up with that of your family? Where would he be most comfortable? The decision between public and private education isn't as clear-cut as it was years ago. Choosing your child's education is an important decision. Make sure you choose your child's school for the right reasons.

Nanny Tip

Allow your child to express her thoughts about her school preferences. You certainly don't have to heed her advice, but if she knows her feelings were thoughtfully heard, it will make your decision much easier for her to swallow.

Private School

There are several benefits to attending a private school. Usually, the class sizes are smaller and the teacher-to-student ratio is higher. Teachers also have more flexibility to be creative in their teaching methods and styles. Since private schools aren't held to the same national standards as public schools, they don't have to do all the required paperwork or focus more on test scores than actual learning, which frees up more time for classroom instruction. Private schools also tend to have more parent involvement and a great spirit of volunteerism.

In almost all studies, private-school students tend to outperform public-school students on standardized tests. However, a recent study by Christopher Lubienski and Sarah Theule Lubienski, education profes-

The National Council for Private School Accreditation (www.ncpsa.org) serves as the review panel over all of the accrediting organizations and is a great resource to help you learn about the accreditation process of private schools.

sors at the University of Illinois at Urbana-Champaign, found that this may be more of a reflection of drawing "students from wealthier and more educated families, rather than because they're better at bolstering student achievement."[1]

That said, the cost of private education is one obvious disadvantage of private schools. Another possible drawback: if your child is the only kid on the block who doesn't attend the neighborhood public school, it may make it more difficult for him to build backyard friendships. Private-school schedules don't always match up with the public-school system, so it can be more of a challenge to get your child involved with neighborhood playdates and city recreational sports and programs. Private schools are also usually more of a distance from the home, which calls for an extra effort to make the commute. And private schools often have less diversity in the student body than public schools, so your child may not have as much opportunity to interact with those from different social, economic, and racial groups.

Many people mistakenly think that attending private school from the early years is a guaranteed ticket into an Ivy League university. Some parents even believe that private schools protect their children from the outside world, since public schools (they think) can't stop harassment, violence, or "bad" kids from influencing their child. Others choose private education because they believe that it offers a superb learning environment that will give their child an unparalleled advantage. Parents who choose to send their kids to private religious schools appreciate the fact that their child will be taught from their own personal perspective.

To some degree, private education may offer advantages over the public-school system, but private schooling is no guarantee that your child will receive a superior education or mingle with any "better" kids. It is, however, fairly guaranteed that your family's cash flow will be stretched unless you're among the affluent. One friend of mine sent her children to a local, private Christian school at great sacrifice only to find, to her hurt and disappointment, that the kids who went there were more interested in cliques and social status than in showing Christlike, unconditional love and acceptance.

> ### *Nanny Tip*
> Be sure to pay a visit to each of your school choices. Ask if there are any parents who might be willing to share their experience with other potential school applicants.

With fear and trembling, the next year she enrolled her four children in the local public schools and braced for the worst. To her surprise and delight, her kids loved the public schools and had highly qualified teachers (many of whom turned out to be fair and loving Christians), and all her children graduated from this small-town school to go on to major universities and fulfilling careers. With the money saved on enormous tuition bills, the family could afford to go on memorable family vacations and send some of their teens on short-term mission trips, Christian camps, and other activities that ensured their exposure to other kids in fun and life-enriching religious environments.

Are the benefits of private schooling worth the financial strain it puts on the average family? Unless you are in a very poorly run school district or there are some other unique factors at play, I lean toward enrolling children in the public-school system (with plenty of exposure to positive religious experiences in other ways) for the reasons we'll discuss next.

Public School

I'll be the first to admit that all public schools and systems aren't the same. They vary from town to town and state to state. But even though they vary, they are all held to state and/or national standards. Some schools will invariably fall below national set standards, some will meet the standards, and some will exceed them—but at least there is a measuring stick by which to compare and evaluate. The No Child Left Behind Act, initiated by President George W. Bush, has created higher standards and methods of accountability that have improved the quality of our nation's public schools. (You can research the school systems in your area by viewing the No Child Left Behind school report cards at http://nces.ed.gov/nations-reportcard/states/.)

A 2003 study from the National Center for Education Statistics concluded that public-school teachers often tend to be more qualified than private-school teachers. In 1999 through 2000, the study found that 47 percent of public-school teachers had a master's degree or higher, when in comparison only 35 percent of private-school teachers held the same degrees.[2]

Public schools, because they are often bigger and more diverse and have more resources, can offer extracurricular activities in a wide variety of areas. Although financial support for these programs has been waning over the years, schools have

Public-School Resources

Author, speaker, and educator Cheri Fuller has written several great books that will help you maximize your child's learning experiences. Visit her Web site at www.cherifuller.com.

Cynthia Tobias has written several thought-provoking books on education, is an expert on learning styles, and gives insight into the public-school experience. Visit her Web site at www.applest.com.

always seemed to find a way to make these activities happen—whether it be through charging nominal fees or by having intramural rather than competitive programs.

Research and statistics aside, in my opinion, the choice between public or private education comes down to an environmental question rather than an educational one. All things considered, what's the best fit for your child? Which school system provides an environment that can most support (or at least not tear down) the family code you have built?

If family time and community involvement are major components of your family's code, you might want to find out which school will allow your kids more free time with less stressful schedules. If your child needs more challenge to keep from getting bored, you may want to consider a school with more rigorous academics. If your child has learning challenges or special needs, your first priority needs to be finding a school that has the resources to help your child feel most successful. If religious training is an important core value in your family, does public school make sense? So much depends on your child.

Ideally, we all want to send our kids out as lights to shine in the world. Some kids are able to do that in the public schools—they stay firm in their faith and values, prosper in a secular environment, and influence the culture around them for good. But there are other children (perhaps in the same family) who simply are too sensitive or easily swayed by peers, and these kids may need an alternative. Watch your children and notice where they tend to bloom and blossom best. Each one has unique needs.

Homeschooling

Another education option available for parents to consider is homeschooling. According to the National Home Education Research Institute, homeschooling is the "fastest growing form of education."[3]

Homeschooling advocate Dr. Brian Ray reports that "the most in-depth nationwide study on home education across the United States collected data on 5,402 students from 1,657 families. Homeschool students' academic achievement, on average, was significantly above that of public-school students. In addition, the home educated did well even if their parents were not certified teachers and if the state did not highly regulate homeschooling."[4]

In addition, parents who choose to homeschool choose this educational option because it provides them with a sense of security: they have control over the educational and social experiences of their children. Many parents want to give their children a solid foundation of religious training, and they enjoy teaching their children in an environment that makes all of life a learning experience. Moms can take their kids to the grocery store to teach hands-on budgeting, meal planning, nutrition information, and math. Dads can teach measuring, basic geometry, and design with

Homeschooling Resources

The National Home Education Network offers up-to-date homeschooling resources and information on its comprehensive Web site (www.nhen.org).

Jon Shemitz shares his experiences and resources as a homeschool dad on his Web site, Jon's Homeschool Resources (www.midnightbeach.com/hs/).

HEARTS—Homeschoolers: Education Assisting and Reaching Out Through Service (www.h-e-a-r-t-s.org) is an organization dedicated to coordinating home-educating families.

Vicki Caruana (www.applesandchalkdust.com) has authored several books for homeschooling parents. Caruana offers the advantage of having taught her children at home but also having been a teacher in the public-school system, so she brings a real balance to the subject. Check out her books *The Organized Home Schooler*, *The ABCs of Home Schooling*, and The Home Schooler's Guide to . . . series.

hands-on learning in the garage workshop. History lessons can be brought to life by taking family vacations to Civil War sites or walking the Freedom Trail in Boston.

Some parents are well suited to teaching their own children, so homeschooling works well, especially in the early years. Some parents, however, love the *idea* of homeschooling their children but in reality are overwhelmed by combining the task of being teacher with mothering (or fathering), running the home, being a wife (or husband), and having some time alone to refuel. If you decide to check into homeschooling as an option, do your research carefully and get all the support you can from other homeschooling families in your area who often do joint field trips and even share in teaching some specific classes.

My personal view on homeschooling is that I am glad it is a viable option for parents today, especially in a situation where neither public nor private school is able to educate your child in a manner that you believe is best. I have seen situations where a child who was lagging academically and socially in a regular school environment was taken out of the situation and homeschooled for a year or two, resulting in a remarkable change. By giving their child a stabilizing time apart from the school environment, the parents often found their child emotionally and academically better prepared for regular classroom situations at a later date. I applaud the fact that we have freedom of choice and that parents can evaluate their child's needs and make the best decision for that child.

That said, I have observed, as you probably have, too, that there are some homeschooled kids who simply don't seem quite normal socially, who appear much more at ease with adults than kids their own age. It's obvious that they lack a certain sense of being a normal kid, especially when it comes to relationships with other children. For this reason, I think it is very important that homeschooled children get plenty of chances to socialize with kids their own age in a variety of healthy settings. If you are considering the homeschool route, you need to be sure that you have the energy and resources to take field trips with other groups of kids, get involved with local sports or other activities offered in your community, and make every opportunity for your child to build lasting friendships.

Although parents and organizations have made a conscious effort to develop curriculum and accountability plans for homeschooled students, there is no real standard set of checks and balances for homeschooling, such as is provided by the public school. There is no one sitting in the learning area of homeschooled children making sure that the time allotted to each area of learning is being met. There is no additional support for the child or the teacher (unless you proactively seek it out).

Taking on the educational responsibility of your child is a huge commitment, since you already have so many other areas where you need to be at the top of your game, especially if you have babies or toddlers at home as well. My best advice for you is to be sure, before you commit to homeschooling, that you aren't spreading yourself too thin. Not all personality types are cut out for the job of academically educating their own kids, no matter the convincing words of some homeschooling advocates. Don't be guilted into homeschooling your kids by misguided individuals who believe that the only true and godly way to educate your kids is to do it yourself at home.

A final word on homeschooling: Although we all want to protect our children from negative outside influences and from anything that would hurt their feelings or challenge their values, teaching children (at an appropriate time and age) how to deal with the normal ups and downs of life is an important part of helping them grow up. You want to allow your children to experience some conflict, some challenges, some questions, and some opposition in this life. As long as they feel safe to talk it over with you at home and work through the process of getting along with others, interacting with the real world is a vitally important part of maturing and gaining self-confidence.

Charter School—The Best of All Worlds?

Charter schools have been quickly spreading across the country as an innovative type of public schooling. Born out of Minnesota in 1991, this private public school seems like a foreign concept until you really grasp what this movement is about. I'll do my best to share some basic information, but the real charter-school experts reside at www.charterfriends.org, where through a grant from the Department of U.S. Education, they developed a publication entitled "The Charter School Experience."[5]

Charter schools are nonsectarian public schools that are released from many regulations placed on traditional public schools. The "charter" refers to the contract that establishes the mission, goals, and measures of success that the school will use. The contract is established between the granting party, usually a local school board, and the operators of the facility. The exact definition of a charter school can vary from state to state (forty states currently have laws regarding charter schools), but according to the Education Commission of the States, "Charter schools are semi-autonomous public schools, founded by educators, parents, community groups or private organizations that operate under a written contract with a state, district or other entity. This contract, or charter, details how the school will be organized and managed, what students will be taught and expected to achieve, and how success will be measured. Many charter schools enjoy freedom from rules and regulations affecting other public schools, as long as they continue to meet the terms of their charters. Charter schools can be closed for failing to satisfy these terms."[6]

Parents, educators, and community members choose charter schools because they can be involved in their development and operation. They help set the educational vision and goals and map the plan of how they wish to achieve those goals. They can use the approaches and philosophies that they feel fit their vision.

Charter schools give parents, students, and educators a choice as an educational team effort. Parents get to create new opportunities for their children through starting and participating in the development of charter schools. Educators get the freedom to teach as they see fit and to apply the methods that they feel work, since they don't have to follow state curriculum and methods. And students benefit from the smaller class sizes and the enthusiasm of the teachers, parents, and community who are responsible for ensuring a thriving educational experience.

If it sounds too good to be true, is it? Parents, students, and teachers involved in charter schools say not. They seem satisfied. Charter schools are proving to be academically successful and are continuing to pop up all over the nation as a people-pleasing alternative form of education.

Help Their Lights Shine

Regardless of the educational route you choose, how can you encourage your child to let her light shine in a world that can so easily be dark and confusing?

Standing up for what you believe can be hard, especially when your beliefs are different from others'. It is important to remind your children why you have family standards. Let them know that there may be times they'll be judged for their personal values, and it won't be fair or fun. Encourage your children to be the example to their peers, to be the light that can provide direction to others, to choose the alternate route when faced with a situation where "everyone else is

Here are the top ten things to know about charter schools, according to Leadership for Quality Education (www.lqe.org).

Charter schools are:
1. publicly funded
2. not vouchers for private schools
3. open to all students
4. pioneers and innovators in public education
5. meeting parents' needs
6. appealing places to work for teachers
7. committed to improving public education
8. operated by an exciting array of nonprofit groups
9. playing an important part in school reform
10. demonstrating a record of student achievement

doing it." Encourage them to respect others who believe differently and always to treat others the way they want to be treated.

Learning to stand up for your values is especially important when your child faces opposition from others who don't respect her beliefs or embrace her differences. Not everyone likes us all the time. Not everyone always agrees with us. That is a universal truth. Since challenges and opposition are inevitable, you need to provide your child with the tools to handle these situations with grace.

Role-play situations with your child. Pretend a classmate says, "I don't want to play with you because you can't play the video games I like. Your parents must think you are better than us." Give her some sample responses: "I'm hurt that you don't want to play. I really wanted to play with you. There are lots of other things we can do, and my parents just have different rules than your parents. It doesn't mean we think our family is better or worse; it is just how we work. Maybe your family has some rules that our family doesn't follow. It's no big deal."

Give your child ample opportunity to express her feelings. Encourage her to share openly with you, and validate her by saying, "Yes, I can see how that would hurt."

Give your child a safe environment to take risks in so that you can help her through her successes and failures. If you prepare her for taking risks, she'll know what to do when the time comes to face them alone. Invite children to your house to play, observe their interactions, and be there to model appropriate behavior when things start to go off track. Praise your child when things do stay on track.

Remind your child that people will always let her down (but God won't!) and that learning from these experiences is part of growing up. Assure her she is not a failure and that she should never give up, because tomorrow is a new day. Share a time when you experienced opposition from a peer and how you lived through it.

Encourage your child to be the example. Teach her always to treat others the way that she wants to be treated. The Golden Rule is as applicable to your child today as it was when this standard for how to live with others was advocated centuries ago.

Show your child that she is unconditionally valued and loved. If you consistently affirm your unconditional love for your child, when she begins to question the love others have for her, her inner self won't be shaken (or at least won't be destroyed). Write her a little note or put a card that says, "I'm so proud of you!" on her pillow for her to find at night or in her lunch box for her to find at school. Give her a surprise bear hug for no reason except to say, "Have I told you today what a great kid you are?"

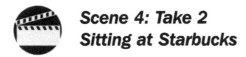

Scene 4: Take 2
Sitting at Starbucks

MARY, *to the Monday Moms Coffee Club.* So it's almost March 10, and you know what that means: we'll know if Lucy got into private school.

KATRINA. Well, if you ask me, the public schools here are just fine. They are what you make of them, and if you stay involved and on top of things, the kids do just as well. They aren't for everyone, I guess, but they've been wonderful for us.

PATRICIA, *sighing.* Well, ladies, I'm glad I don't have to worry about that. The charter-school planning has been going so well. It's like a private public school—all the perks and none of the payments. We signed up, and I can't wait to see how Katie does. We decided that the potential benefits are worth the risk of trying something new.

KATRINA. Mary, how many schools did you apply to, and what made you choose them?

MARY. Well, you know, we have the backup private school, the decent private school, and the ultimate private school. But really . . . we are hoping she gets into the decent one. It seems to be the best match for her personality type and learning style. The public schools in our district aren't thriving. I don't have the time to dedicate to enroll her in the charter school, never mind the patience for homeschooling. For us, a well-rounded education that lines up with our family code was the best choice, and in our case that happens to be the decent private school.

WENDY. Two of mine are going back to the public school this year, but Misty was in tears most of last semester. My husband and I sense she will do better with some one-on-one time with me as she gets back on track emotionally, socially, and academically. So I'm homeschooling her. Pray for us!

Ladies, joining in. You bet!

PATRICIA. Wouldn't it be great to pray for all of our kids, their teachers, and their school experience all year? I know we would love that sort of support!

(The moms around the table raise their lattes in mutual support and agreement.)

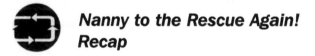

Nanny to the Rescue Again! Recap

What was the significance of this Coffee Club chatter?

1. *The educational decision was based on what was best for the child.* "We explored our options and made the right choice for our family and our child."

2. *The educational and family values were consistent.* "We are looking for an educational route that matches up with what we believe."

3. *The individual choices were respected.* What is right for your child is what matters, and it doesn't mean that the same situation is the right choice for another.

4. *The choices were made for the right reasons.* Getting into an Ivy League university wasn't the basis for the school choice. Careful consideration of the pros and cons of each option left each set of parents with the outcome that was right for their family.

5. *There was a mutual show of support for the complexity of the educational decisions that needed to be made.* Each mom trusted that the others were making the best choice for her personality, belief system, and child. Unlike the moms in the first example, this group of moms showed respect for one another.

CHAPTER FIVE

LEARNING LOGIC, HOMEWORK HASSLES, AND TEACHER TACTICS

 Scene 5: Take 1
After School

MOM. Come on, James, you have to get your homework done.

JAMES. I don't want to do it now.

MOM. Well, kiddo, it's not an option, so let's get crackin'.

JAMES. Mom, I'll do it later.

MOM. When is later?

JAMES. After dinner. I just don't want to do it now.

MOM, *after dinner but before bedtime.* James! Did you finish your homework?
Silence.

MOM. James? (*She looks in his room and finds her son asleep on his bed with his school reading book on his chest.*)

D o you have a daughter who can't seem to remember anything you tell her to do but thrives on written lists? How about a son whose eyes glaze over when you try to teach him the alphabet, but he learned to tie a knot in six different ways in no time at all as long as he could touch and handle the rope? Or perhaps you have a child who finds reading dull and laborious but loves to be read to or listen to books on tape.

There is a brilliant child locked inside every student.
—Marva Collins

The Three Learning Styles

One of the most insightful, practical, and helpful outcomes of educational research in the last few years is the realization that we all learn best in different ways. There are three basic ways we take in information, and it will help you and your child's teacher tremendously to find out which style of learning works best for your child. Most teachers are aware of the three learning styles, but it might be helpful for you to pass on what you've observed about your particular child's best style—and whenever possible, the teacher may be able to adjust her lesson to help your child absorb new information.

Visual Learners: *Learn Through Seeing*

These learners need to see the teacher's body language and facial expression to fully understand the content of a lesson. They tend to prefer sitting at the front of the classroom to avoid visual obstructions (e.g., people's heads). They may think in pictures and learn best from visual displays including diagrams, illustrated textbooks, overhead transparencies, videos, flip charts, and handouts. During a lecture or classroom discussion, visual learners often prefer to take detailed notes to absorb the information.

Auditory Learners: *Learn Through Listening*

Auditory learners learn best through verbal lectures, discussions, talking things through, and listening to what others have to say. Auditory learners interpret the underlying meanings of speech through listening to tone of voice, pitch, speed, and other nuances. Written information may have little meaning until it is heard. These learners often benefit from reading text aloud and using a tape recorder.

Tactile/Kinesthetic Learners: *Learn Through Moving, Doing, and Touching*

Tactile/kinesthetic learners learn best through a hands-on approach, actively exploring the physical world around them. They may find it hard to sit still for long periods and may become distracted by their need for activity and exploration.

Be Aware of Learning Disabilities

There are also some learning disabilities you should be generally aware of, just in case you think your child may suffer from one of them, thus keeping him from performing at his best. Typical learning difficulties include dyslexia (a language and reading disability), dyscalculia (specific problems with math), and dysgraphia (a writing disorder resulting in illegibility). These learning difficulties are sometimes complicated by related disorders such as attention deficit/hyperactivity disorder.

Every student can learn,
just not on the same day,
or the same way.
—George Evans

One of the best advocacy Web sites for information for parents and teachers on learning disorders is Learning Disabilities Association of America (www.ldaamerica.us). You will find an abundance of resources and specific support from your own state on this Web site.

Handling Homework Hassles

Another problem that often leaves your child (and you) at the point of tears is handling after-school homework, particularly if your active child is reluctant to come home from sitting in school all day, only to sit some more and do still more schoolwork. Every child needs time to run off energy, get a nutritious snack, and play or lollygag or nap before diving right back into filling in the blanks or doing the multiplication table. Notice when your child is most able to focus, sit still, and complete his homework. Timing is everything, and that timing varies with your child's temperament and body clock.

Here are a few guidelines and tricks that might help halt the hassles of doing homework.

Do homework at the same time. Be consistent in your child's daily homework routine. The workload increases as he gets older, so make sure that he has enough time to get all his homework done without rushing. Some kids prefer "getting it over with" as soon as they walk in the door. Others prefer tackling their homework after dinner when their tummy tanks register full. Choose a time that works best for your child.

> ### *Nanny Tip*
>
> End homework hassles by having your children take part in designing the homework area. Selecting paper, pencils, and other office supplies in colors and styles your children like will provide incentive to be in the area. Allow them a corkboard they can decorate any way they wish. Don't laugh when you start seeing cutouts from magazines of their latest crushes or "I Love Chase" tacked firmly at eye level!

Do homework in the same place. Have a set place where your child does his homework. A nicely lit, quiet place that is specifically designated for homework works well. Let him choose how it is decorated. Kids will flock to an "office" of their own, especially when Mom and Dad leave special surprises in a desk drawer for work completed: a pack of sugarless gum, a granola bar, a written pass good for a movie over the weekend, and so on.

Pace the projects. Teach your child not to wait until the last minute when assignments come up. Help him break projects and assignments into manageable, bite-size pieces so he won't choke.

Do homework with other students. Encourage your child to start a homework club where some of their friends agree to do their homework at the same time each day, thus eliminating phone calls or TV that would cut into that time. One day a week, older kids can even meet at the library after school. Or you could be brave and have a weekly homework day, where the homework gang can meet at your house after school to do their homework and end the workday with a fun and fabulous dinner. Bonus: grade-school girls (and some guys) generally love to help cook, and preadolescent guys will leave you with no leftovers!

Working Through Teacher Tangles

Have you ever worked for a boss with whom you just didn't click? One who seemed to do everything contrary to your liking? One who had systems in place that made no logical sense to you?

If you've ever asked yourself, "Does my boss like me?" "Why doesn't she choose me for a promotion?" or, "Why does he insist on leading in this nonproductive fashion?" then you know what it feels like to lose the ability to focus on your job. Your anxiety has blocked the path to your brain and productivity. I know that there have been times I have been so preoccupied with wondering, "What was wrong with *my* way?" that I almost lost track of the task at hand.

As adults, we know the skills to help us shake off distractions and get back on task—most of the time. However, a child doesn't have this high level of reasoning ability, and when he finds himself at odds with the teacher ("the boss" of the classroom), his resulting anxiety may stop all learning.

Personality Clashes

Most likely at some point your child will come across a teacher with whom he just doesn't click. Teachers, since they're human beings, bring into the classroom their own personalities, prejudices, and preferred methods of teaching, discipline, and interaction with children.

Most teachers are exceptional people. I, for one, think that any adult who teaches small children in a closed classroom all week and is still standing and smiling by Friday afternoon deserves some sort of medal of honor (or at least a medal of endurance). Teachers are often exhausted and overwhelmed. But like nannies, teachers who are truly called to their work love what they do and could not imagine a more rewarding career. Next to parenthood (and nannyhood), teaching and inspiring children is probably the greatest job on earth!

Most teachers really do want to see your child succeed in every way, and they know how to adjust their teaching style to the personality of anyone in the class. Last year, I remember commenting to my charge Fraser's kindergarten teacher that she was a great personality match for him. They were able to build a bond because she responded to him in such a way that he understood she cared, but she wouldn't tolerate less than his best. Her actions toward him gave him confidence in who he was in her eyes—a bright, enthusiastic kindergartener with special and unique talents and gifts. He blossomed under this kind of attitude. Then, without thinking, I said, "Your style would have been more of an adjustment for his twin brother, Austin, because he needs lots of extra nurturing, loving care." She was quick to disagree. "I feel confident Austin would have been fine, too, because I adjust to all of my students . . . and them to me. I've never had a child not like me."

She was probably right, and my perceptions were probably wrong. Sometimes it surprises parents how well their kids adapt to teachers who are very different from them. The good news is that kids need experience with a wide variety of personality types in order to mature socially. So don't panic just because you meet your child's teacher and assume that she is so different from you or your spouse that there is going to be trouble in the classroom. You might just be very pleasantly surprised to watch your child adapt and blossom with a variety of teacher types.

Actuality Versus Perception

When people talk about personality clashes between students and teachers, it usually comes up because of certain actions—or perceived actions—that the teacher has taken toward or against a student.

Favoritism, singling out a child, picking on a child, and exclusion are all examples that involve both actual and perceived points of conflict. Sometimes a child will resent a teacher and think of her as the "bad guy" because there is an increase in homework or classroom responsibilities. The child perceives this as a personal attack, even though the entire class may have the same assignment. (As the school year goes along, generally, the workload increases.)

Does your child complain of being overlooked? Before assuming this is intentional on the part of the teacher, realize that seat arrangements in the classroom have a lot to do with which child gets attention. Maybe the teacher will call on the child in seat number four more than any other, not because of the child who's sitting there but because that seat is directly in her line of vision. It's a good idea to talk to your child's teacher about her feelings, but don't ever assume that the teacher is purposely trying to hurt or neglect your child, especially before you get the whole story. In fact, a great way to handle this discussion is by saying, "I know you have twenty-five kids in your class, so there is no way you can know everything that goes on in each of their minds. I just wanted to let you know that Jessica is feeling a bit overlooked when she raises her hand to answer a question. Is there perhaps a place where she might sit where it would be easier to see her hand go up? Or could you maybe rotate the desks each week?"

The best teachers will not label your child, nor will they adopt a previous teacher's label. For example, if Samuel was labeled a playground bully in first grade, word may get around the teacher's lounge and his second-grade teacher may give special attention to him on the playground. Perhaps when Samuel threw the ball too hard for the first time in dodgeball, he was taken out of the game completely, whereas another child, with a reputation for being more compliant, would just have to miss a turn.

Whether or not a teacher intended to be unfair isn't the point. The point is that your child *perceives* that he is being singled out unfairly, and that is the issue a parent has to handle . . . delicately.

Relationships Affect Academics

In any relationship, how children see themselves through the eyes of an adult impacts their attitudes about themselves, which in turn affects their behavior. If a child feels that he is liked and well received by the teacher, he is going to participate in class actively. If he feels his opinions are valued, he will share them. If he is comfortable in his environment and with those around him, it will show.

On the other hand, if a child feels she is not liked or valued, she may not take the risk of speaking up and sharing her thoughts or opinions because she doesn't want to be rejected. If she feels insignificant to the teacher, she will act as if she is. If she feels that she is not valued, she won't contribute.

If a child is not performing at his full academic capacity because of the way he perceives he is being treated, the situation needs to be addressed. His "feeler" will overtake his "thinker"—and very little real learning will take place until your child feels the emotional safety required for the brain to function well.

When Conflicts Arise

When conflicts arise between your child and the teacher, they need to be resolved—as soon as possible. As Barney Fife would say on the *Andy Griffith Show*, "Nip it, nip it, nip it!" When you notice that your child isn't enthusiastic about class, his grades slip, or he is avoiding talking about or even going to school, you have reason to be concerned.

As soon as the initial concern sets in, begin to ask your child some open-ended questions: "Tell me about school." "Talk to me about your classmates." "What is your teacher like?" Hopefully these questions, asked in a relaxed manner, will open the channels of communication. If your child is a fairly good communicator, he'll have no trouble sharing that he doesn't like his teacher because of x, y, or z, or that a classmate is giving him trouble. If your child does express that he feels he is being treated unfairly or that his teacher doesn't like him or is singling him out in some negative way, first try to figure out where these thoughts came from. How your child perceives what is going on is of more concern than who is at fault.

Here are some things for you to remember when your child shares his negative feelings about school or a teacher.

Don't take sides—be objective. It's hard not to jump into the "rescuing your child" mode, but before you do, try to look at the situation objectively. Be a compassionate but impartial information gatherer. Validate your child's feelings without tearing down the teacher.

Schedule a conference or meeting. It's much better to have the teacher's attention one-on-one when she is relaxed and unpressured, rather than grabbing her in the hallway before school when she is already busy and focused on getting her classroom ready.

Share your child's perception with the teacher in a nonjudgmental way. "I want you to know that I'm not blaming you in any way, but I just want you to know what James is feeling and expressing to me at home, so you and he can come to a better understanding—and he can feel happier and be able to focus on his work. For some reason, James feels as though you don't like him. I'm sure that's not the case, but that doesn't change the way he feels." Then kindly explain what is happening, from James's perspective, to cause these feelings.

Ask for—and offer—suggestions. "Do you have any ideas on what we can do to change the way James perceives how you feel about him? Could you write James a

'Great work!' note the next time he makes an attempt at a challenging activity?" Also ask if there is anything that you, as a parent, might be able to do to help.

Follow up. Thank the teacher for her time and let her know that you'll keep her updated on how James is feeling. Notice if his attitude or grades change after there is a conscious effort on the teacher's part to be sensitive to James's feelings.

Support Your Local Teacher

If you are a Christian mom who would like to join other moms in being a positive influence by praying for and encouraging your child's teacher, check out the nonprofit organization called Moms In Touch (www.momsintouch.org). Two or more moms (or grandmas or caretakers) meet for one hour each week to pray for their children, their children's teachers, and administrators.

Another way to encourage your child's teacher is to send uplifting notes or gifts that she can use in the classroom. Many teachers have to buy things like stickers or classroom treats and educational toys out of their own very limited personal budget. Ask your child's teacher for a "dream list" of things she'd love to have in the classroom but cannot buy within the school budget limitations. Pass it around to other parents who might want to contribute or do a private fund-raiser.

Volunteer to help on field trips or for room parties, to take down bulletin boards, or to prepare special projects. Bring a surprise plate of cookies on special occasions. Volunteer to share a special gift you may have, such as playing an instrument, telling stories, or teaching a craft from a foreign country. You'll not only get to know the teacher and your child's friends, but your child will beam with pride at having you there.

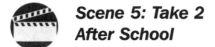

Scene 5: Take 2
After School

MOM. Come on, James, you have to get your homework done.

JAMES. I don't want to do it now.

MOM. Well, kiddo, I understand that you don't want to come home after school and do more schoolwork, but it's not an option, so let's get crackin'.

JAMES. Mom, I'll do it later.

MOM. James, you know the rules. You have a half hour to do what you wish after school, then it's homework time. We've tried it right after school, before dinner, and after dinner, and this routine seems to work best. So hop to it, buddy. Your office awaits you!

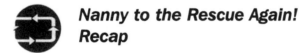

Nanny to the Rescue Again!
Recap

What did this mom do to take the hassles out of homework?

1. *She found a routine that worked.* She tried it different ways and discovered a way that worked best for everyone.

2. *She stuck to the routine.* The schedule wasn't compromised. "We do homework now, not later."

3. *She acknowledged her child's feelings.* "Yeah, having to do schoolwork after school does stink. I understand, but we have to do it anyway."

4. *She taught her child that you have to do what you have to do.* "Some things in life are nonnegotiable. We don't make the school rules, but we have to follow them."

5. *She had prepared a homework haven.* The child had a place that was exclusively set up to accommodate his schoolwork.

CHAPTER SIX

PLANNING PERFECT PLAYDATES

 Scene 6: Take 1
In the Pickup Line at School

MARIAH. Can you come over and play at my house today?

ASHLEY. Sure! Can we do some art projects?

MARIAH. Let's watch a movie and eat popcorn first. That will be more fun!

ASHLEY. Yeah, I love great movies. *Mary Poppins* and *Stuart Little* are
my favorites.

MARIAH. *Miss Congeniality* was so good. It's my favorite! We can watch that!

ASHLEY, *enthusiastically yelling when she sees her mom coming to get her from the
pickup line.* Mom, can I go to Mariah's today?

MOM. Um, OK, I guess. Let's ask her mom. Which one is she again?

So Mariah wants to play with your daughter Ashley, this time at her house. When she's at your house, you don't mind, because everyone has to play by your house rules, under your supervision. Even though Mariah is raised a bit differently than your daughter and operates under a different family code—one that doesn't exactly match up with yours—you take comfort in knowing that when she's on your turf, you have at least some control.

When Mariah uses language that you deem inappropriate, you can point it out and offer correction in front of your child, reinforcing what is and is not acceptable in your home. When Mariah wants to play a game such as "kill the king"— one that she's made up, of course, because you only have games in your home that you approve of—you can help your child say no and suggest an alternative.

So what happens now, when your child is invited to a friend's house—one where you may not know the parents or the house rules? Or maybe one where you don't even really know the child? How do you handle these situations?

Ground Rules for Playdates

As with anything else, being prepared goes a long way. One of the things I have found helpful is having a basic set of rules that determines *who* my charges play with, *when* they are ready to play with them, and *where* the playdate takes place.

Who Your Child Plays With

Chances are your child will look for friends who have the same interests—ones who enjoy playing the same games and talking about the same things as she does. Then again, there is the old but true adage: opposites attract. It is not uncommon for a child to seek out a buddy who is her complete opposite. This could be good news or bad news!

Maybe your daughter is not a thrill seeker and would never jump off a desk at school, but with a friend she finds it easier to take part. Not so good. If this is consistently the case, you will probably have to limit the amount of time your child spends with another child who influences your kid toward trouble. On the other hand, perhaps your child is a shrinking violet, struggling with shyness in social settings. An outgoing friend may rub off on your child and give her much-needed courage to bloom and grow.

A mom pal of mine had a little girl, Rachel, who was painfully shy. The day her daughter started first grade, my friend got a note from the teacher that said, "I'm really worried that Rachel is so shy, we may have a real problem in communicating in the classroom. When I call on her to answer a question, she simply nods or shakes her head but cannot seem to get the words to come out of her mouth."

My friend didn't know what to do—and then an answer came. A humdinger of an outgoing child, aptly nicknamed Cricket, befriended her daughter. Cricket didn't know the meaning of the word *timid* and simply pulled Rachel into the "whoosh!" of her outgoing personality. Cricket introduced Rachel to a group of friends, made Rachel laugh out loud with her theatrical antics, planned fun outings and creative games for the two of them . . . and little by little Rachel's shyness simply disappeared. In fact, my friend was laughing as she shared, "My shy little girl, whom I feared might never come out of her shell, is now a senior in high school and just gave a hilarious speech to five hundred high school students at a student council convention. Guess who was clapping and laughing the hardest—on the front row? Yes, her faithful, funny friend, Cricket."

"As iron sharpens iron, so one man sharpens another," the proverb says.[1] Your child will probably have (and need) a variety of friends for different reasons. She may or may not have one best friend, but try to teach her to look for the best in all her friends and enjoy what they bring to her life.

When Your Child Is Ready to Play

I believe in building a strong social circle for children from the get-go. I remember a time years ago when a group of us nannies were hanging out in the park, blankets and toys spread out among six or eight babies. It was great to see the children observe one another and learn the laws of social interaction firsthand. For example, if you pull the hair of the person to your right, most likely your right hand will get chomped on.

The great thing about playdates in the preschool years is that when a playdate is planned, it is generally for the child *and* the parent or caregiver. It is a given that you will be there and be part of the event. You will supervise your child while the other participants supervise theirs. You take turns at one another's homes and enjoy watching the kids grow together in a safe, supervised environment.

As you make your way into the school years, you quickly learn (or at least I did) that this isn't always the case. I remember the first time my charge was invited on a playdate in kindergarten. When I responded to the invitation with a familiar, "Sure, we'll be glad to come!" the mom said, "Oh, I just assumed he'd come alone."

Kids socially mature at different ages. Some children may be ready to have their first playdate without you when they are in preschool. Others may be ready when they are in first or second grade. It's also true that parents (and nannies) have different levels of comfort with leaving their child with an unfamiliar person in an unfamiliar environment. It takes time to build a sense of trust and security in the person who will be temporarily responsible for your child. You need to be sure that you can leave your child in the home of another with confidence.

Fortunately, when our first solo invitation came, I had already had the rule in place (at least in my head) that my charges wouldn't be going alone on playdates until I knew the family, the house rules, and how the kids played together. My charge and I would also have to have a certain level of comfort with the family and environment before taking that step.

Where the Playdate Should Take Place

First playdates always happen at our house. It's a nonnegotiable with me. OK, yes, it may be because I'm a wee bit of a control freak; but with the kids in my care, I personally would rather err on the side of being overly cautious.

This is my policy because I like the chance to observe firsthand how the kids play together in a one-on-one setting. Do they need organized activities, or do they come up with things to do on their own? Are they into sports or into board games? Is the friend's behavior appropriate, according to our family's standards? If not, is the friend respectful of my correction and willing to follow our house rules? Of course, the parent of the friend is always welcome and encouraged to come along, but I've found that the majority of the time, they prefer not to.

Safe, Supervised Playdates

When children are playing at our house, especially the first time, they are supervised so that if anything unexpected happens, I am there (if needed) to help. My agenda isn't to clean the house while my charge is occupied; it's to oversee the children as they build their friendship. I highly recommend that you don't plan to do anything mind-absorbing the first time or two your child has a new friend over. Plan to be a hands-on mom helping the kids get started on the right foot, and once they are happily playing, do something nearby that allows you to still be attentive to them. Once you know and trust how the children play with each other, you can back off a bit and allow them more freedom out of your sight and hearing.

Kids who visit our home don't get to exercise free rein. Our play area doesn't consist of the entire house; it is limited to the first-floor kitchen and playroom area. This works well because all play areas can easily be seen and supervised. I can see what's happening without hovering over the kids. The kids have the opportunity to play on their own, with the security of knowing I am nearby.

Since our play area is specifically meant for playing, it is a safe place that only has items in it that meet our family standards. The toys are age appropriate, weapons are not allowed, and there is a multitude of educational activities for the kids to enjoy. For example, you won't find toy guns in our toy box or PG-13-rated movies on the DVD shelf. You'll find board games and building sets, coloring books and crafts supplies, and *Mary Poppins, Stuart Little,* and other creative G-rated videos and DVDs.

Just as it's my policy that first playdates are always at our house, it's my policy that I always accompany the kids on first playdates at the home of their friend. It's important for me to know the parents and the rules of the family. I want to know if the children are left to play unsupervised in the basement, or if the playroom is near enough to the kitchen or living room so that the parents can easily check in on the kids. I want to know how the parents discipline their child, or if they discipline at all. I want to know, by observation, if my charge is comfortable in the friend's home environment.

I remember being so glad that I had this policy in place the first time we went to the house of a friend who had a dog. One of my charges was petrified. I'm glad that I was there to see the mom's reaction as she immediately put the dog in its kennel and reassured Austin that the dog wouldn't be let out until after the playdate was over and he had gone home. I was there to see her follow through with what she said and attentively nurture my child back to serenity. Her quick and loving reaction built my trust and comfort level.

I also feel it's important to be familiar and comfortable with the environment that your child will be playing in. Are there dangerous areas in the house? Are there weapons in the home? Are there violent video games that you don't want your child playing? If so, you can make a specific request before permitting your daughter to play at the friend's home. "Ashley can come play, but I prefer that she not play video games." The parents probably won't question you further, but if they do, just say, "My spouse and I have a policy that we only allow our kids to play video games that we've seen and approved, so it's just easier to ask that our kids do something else when visiting. Avoids the hassle factor."

When Values Collide

When attending playdates, you'll run across families who have the same policies as yours in place. When this is the case, it all works out quite nicely. You share the same values, have a similar family code, and have mutually comfortable environments that set the stage for a great deal of future playdates to come. Most likely, you'll end up becoming family friends.

The time will also come when things aren't so ideal. The family may have a completely different way of doing things. That family's idea of a playdate may be for the kids to sit alone in a TV room, watching a PG-13 movie and eating unlimited amounts of candy. You may not have any issue with the friend of your child, but the family dynamics and environment cause you concern. The level of supervision of the kids may not satisfy you. In these situations, the easiest route to resolving the issue is to limit playdates to your home or to neutral territory, such as at a playground or in a museum.

I have also run into, although only once, a child with whom I absolutely felt that having a playdate would not work out at all. The child's family code seemed to be completely opposite of ours, my charge wasn't interested in playing with the child, the child's behavior in school and in team sports was consistently inappropriate, and his parents weren't big on any form of discipline. The who and where of the playdate didn't appeal to me or to my charge, so the when wasn't even an issue.

In this case, our policy became "We don't play with children who consistently choose to do inappropriate behavior." It is never a good idea to force a friendship. While you want to encourage your child to treat all others the way she wishes to be treated, you also need to respect her choice of whom she wishes not to befriend.

Evaluating the Invitation

When the time comes that your child makes a new friend, and the natural chain of events leads to developing a friendship outside the four walls of the school, use the following questions to evaluate if the playdate invitation is right for you:

• Does your child mention a school friendship with the other child?
• Does your child express interest in playing with the other child?

- Have you met the other child and/or the parents through class activities or community programs or events?
- Is your child independent? Does she insist on walking into the school or classroom without you?
- Does your child communicate well with adults? Does she express when she is feeling uncomfortable?

If you can answer yes to most of these questions, then chances are your child may be ready to make the move to having playdates without you. (Though your readiness may be a different story!)

When you've decided that it's time to take that step, make an active effort to get to know the parents and the child so that you can develop a mutual level of comfort with one another. Try the following "getting to know you" techniques as you begin to foster your child's friendships:

- Say hello during school drop-off or pickup, and share the interest your child has in playing with the child.
- Ask the mom for a chat over coffee or ask to give her a call to discuss a possible get-together. If you can't catch her in person, look her up in the school directory or phone book, or pass a note to her via the classroom teacher.
- Invite the mom and child over to your home for a playdate. If the mom doesn't want to come along, make sure you ask if the child has any dietary or activity restrictions. If her weekday schedule has no availability, suggest that the first get-together be on a weekend.

> ### Nanny Tip
>
> Teach your child never to ask you for a playdate in front of friends. Make it a policy that if she asks out loud and puts you on the spot, the answer is no. That takes the pressure off you and off the other child's parent.

• Keep the first get-together short. An hour or two after school or on the week-end is plenty of time to get a feel for if the kids enjoy each other's company and if they play well together.

Planning Perfect Playdates

If you set your standards for playdate planning in advance, you can avoid many potential pitfalls that come with the territory.

Prepare for the playdate. Plan the playdate for when you have time, not when you're in a crunch and really wish you would have said no.

Set the rules. Make it clear what behaviors, rooms, and activities are off-limits, but balance those rules with your list of acceptable suggestions for how to behave, where to play, and fun activities.

Provide healthy snacks. After a long day at school, a great snack will turn up the corners of most kids' mouths, even the droopiest ones! Find out the favorites among your kids' friends, and keep a stash for special occasions.

Make the playdate a real playdate. Turn off the TV and shut down the computer. Point the kids to the great outdoors or the game closet instead.

Try to stay out of it. As long as the kids are safe and play within the house rules, let them choose their activities and work out their minor disputes.

Nanny Tip

If you allow your child to snack after school, have a special cupboard called the Playdate Pantry. Make sure it is easy for your child to reach, and stock it with water bottles, juice boxes, crackers, dried fruit, plates, and napkins. Your child will feel like quite the host as the kids help themselves to an afternoon snack.

Creative Playdates

There are lots of fun and creative ways to have playdates with your children and their friends. Don't get stuck in a boring routine—try one of these options!

Playdates on the go. On-the-go outings can be a fun way to have it all—all the fun, none of the mess. They even work when there are different-age siblings who need to come along. Farms, museums, parks, and picnics at playgrounds offer something for everyone.

Nice day out to play. When it's nice outside, it's an outdoors day. Make your backyard inviting. A picnic table, a shady area, some outdoor toys, and a play structure are all worth the investment. For older kids, hanging a basketball hoop or putting up a croquet or badminton set may keep them occupied for hours. The kids will get wiped out without wiping you out. The outdoors provides so many opportunities for imaginary play and physical activity that it is hard to get bored.

Themed playdates. If you are like me and enjoy a bit of structure, themed play-dates are great! Cookie making and decorating, a craft project, LEGO building, and board games are all themed ideas that work well for after-school fun.

The station system. Call me crazy, but the more the merrier! On the days when three or more are gathered for a playdate, I like to set up play stations. We'll have the craft area, where I have a project ready to go (for inexpensive fun projects check out www.orientaltrading.com), and the game area, where I have set out checkers, tic-tac-toe, and other basic two-player games. When I'm really into it, the Twister game comes out, and I won't be the spinner!

Out to lunch. Taking kids out to eat will kill several birds with one entertaining stone. You get everyone fed (which you would have had to do at home anyway) without the hassle of preparation or doing the dishes. You can give all the kids focused attention, and if you go to a family-friendly restaurant, there are often special children's menus that the younger kids can color while the older ones do the puzzles and word searches.

Web searching. Check out www.citysearch.com and search for family-friendly activities and restaurants in your area. If you happen to be in Denver or Chicago (or visit either city while on vacation), check out www.whitefencefarm.com. You'll feel like you've eaten Sunday fried chicken dinner on Grandma's farm, complete with barnyard animals and tree houses and tire swings. Fun for all ages.

Family-friendly magazines and books. Most major cities have parenting magazines with ideas for family activities that are affordable or free of charge. Grocery stores, libraries, and bookstores often carry them near the front of the store. Libraries often carry books with titles like *Best Day Trips for Families* for your local and the surrounding area. It is amazing how often we do this research when we are vacationing but neglect to check out what is in our own cities.

Scene 6: Take 2
In the Pickup Line at School

MARIAH. Can you come over and play at my house today?

ASHLEY. That sounds fun, but I have to ask my mom first. That's the rule. Can we do some art projects if I come?

MARIAH. That's boring. Let's watch a movie and eat popcorn. It's way more fun than dumb art stuff.

ASHLEY. Yes, I love movies, but I'm only allowed to watch the ones my mom lets me. *Stuart Little* and *Mary Poppins* are my favorites.

MARIAH. I love *Miss Congeniality.* It was so good. It's my favorite! We can watch that!

ASHLEY. Here's my mom; let me ask her if we can play. *(Ashley pulls her mom aside and quietly asks if she can go over to Mariah's house and watch a movie.)*

MOM. Honey, you know the rules. First, we need to plan playdates in advance, and second, we'll have to plan a time when I can join you at Mariah's house. You and Mariah played nicely at our house, so let's try to make a date to go over to her house soon.

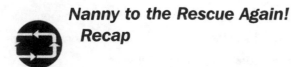

Nanny to the Rescue Again! Recap

How did this mom navigate the politics of playdate planning?

1. *She set clear guidelines with her child about how playdates get planned.* Mom has to know the parents before the kids can play, and playdates need to be planned in advance.
2. *She enforced her policies.* She didn't get put on the spot, because the child knew if she asked in front of the friend, the answer would be no. She also didn't cave in and allow her child to go to the friend's house alone for the first playdate there.
3. *She laid out playdate expectations.* Movies are only for rainy days, and they have to be approved by Mom.
4. *She took the pressure of her child.* She made it OK for Ashley to wait by setting the policy that Mom has to OK the plans before she can make them.

CHAPTER SEVEN

PLAYGROUND POLITICS AND PERSONALITY CONFLICTS

 Scene 7: Take 1
On the Playground

JARED. Let's play keep-away from Kevin!

KEVIN. Why do I always have to be in the middle? It's no fun.

JARED. Come on, knucklehead. It's because you never get the ball and the game lasts long!

KEVIN. Oh, OK. At least I get to play.

JARED. Yup, that's right, Kevin. We let you play! Isn't that cool! Look at Jimmy. We don't let him play at all.

Kevin glances over at Jimmy, who is sitting alone near the playground wall, then sadly nods and takes his place in the middle.

If you think government politics are bad, watch out—you're about to enter a whole new world of politics on the playground. The lies, the betrayals, the entanglements, the drama, the cover-ups—all orchestrated by the minds of those ages twelve and under. In this chapter, we'll explore the cliques, gossip, and catty conversations that are on the daily agenda of our child's life.

Most adults remember what they learned on the playground as much as what they learned in the classroom, if not more. Some good, some bad, some ugly. The middle years are highly social ones: children are learning to make friendships and navigate the ups and downs of relationships. It's a time of social trial and error. It's a time when children are discovering who they are and who their friends are, a time when one day they are best friends with Molly, and the next day, good golly, they never want to speak to Miss Molly again. Resolving conflicts and learning how to deal with hurt feelings are as important a part of growing up as memorizing the multiplication table or learning state history—perhaps much more so.

If you like TV drama, then get ready: you are about to have your own personal reality show, and your child gets to be a star.

Catching Cooties

During the young elementary-school years, a new health epidemic comes on the rise—*cooties*. These "germs" build a concrete divider between the girls and the boys, evidenced by a complete separation of genders on the playground during school recess.

Peaking around grades three and four, this epidemic can be distinctively diagnosed as one observes the school playground. Several small groups of girls will be standing around chatting it up, while the boys will be in one large group, playing a game of soccer or kickball. It's a time when it is just not cool to have friends of the opposite gender. It puts you at risk of becoming infected. The main objective at this age is staying socially healthy by avoiding cooties at all costs, so don't be taken by surprise if Sarah completely ignores Michael, her neighbor and best friend, while on the schoolyard but then comes home and asks if he can come play in your backyard.

By fifth grade, most will outgrow the fear of contamination and slowly begin to acknowledge their interest in the opposite sex. The risk of becoming infected will decrease, because there is now a growing mutual interest in seeing what the girls have to offer the boys and what the boys have to offer the girls. In fact, they seem to want to "catch" whatever it is that the opposite sex possesses. The curiosity factor has been introduced. The girls will now begin to be invited to play in the soccer games, and the boys will be standing along the fence, talking to the girls. (More on encouraging positive, healthy boy-girl friendships in chapter 13.)

Nanny Tip

Although it's an old rule, it's still golden: treat others the way you want to be treated. Make the Golden Rule part of your family's code, and insert it in questions at appropriate moments. "Did you just treat your sister the way you'd want to be treated if you had asked her nicely for a bite of granola bar?"

Lack Social Skills, Lack Friends

Self-confident, funny, assertive kids with a great sense of humor are the ones who seem to emerge as natural leaders. They can seamlessly enter into a group of kids and are often the ones their peers turn to when a problem in the group needs to be resolved. They have no problem walking away when they are in a situation that they simply aren't interested in taking part in. They are leaders, not followers, and often have other kids looking up to them for social guidance. They have developed adequate social skills.

The kids who don't yet possess the same social skills or confidence are the ones who are often unfairly labeled "loners" or "outcasts." These are the kids you will see on the sidelines reading a book or observing the activities of the playground from a distance. They are the ones who appear to be left out or seem to tolerate being treated poorly by their peers. In some instances, it is not that these kids are actually left out; they either enjoy playing the role of observer or haven't yet learned how to gracefully enter into a group and feel awkward when there are more than a few involved in any activity. These kids also may not have the self-confidence to stand up for themselves and will tend to just go with the flow, regardless of the consequences.

Teaching social skills to your child is an important lesson that will provide him with the tools to interact successfully with his peers without succumbing to pressure to head down a rotten path. Here are some tools and skills that will help your child become socially successful.

Self-awareness. Teach your child to identify his feelings, likes, and dislikes and to express them tactfully.

Social cues. Teach your child the importance of nonverbal social communication such as body language, eye contact, facial expressions, and personal space.

Empathy. Teach your child about understanding people and showing compassion to others.

The Golden Rule. Teach your child always to treat others the way he wants to be treated.

Entering in. Teach your child how to enter into a conversation or a group of people. Practice introducing yourself, asking to play, taking turns, and resolving conflicts.

Self-confidence. Take advantage of every opportunity to foster your child's self-confidence. Build him up in such a way that he is confident in who he is.

Role-Play to Teach Social Skills

Role-playing really helps children learn to master social skills. It was one of those things that I didn't believe until I saw it with my own eyes. One day, one of my charges was complaining that another student was making fun of him and he didn't know what to do.

So we practiced. I started by giving him some basic instructions: "When someone says or does something that you don't like, say nicely, 'Please stop. I don't like that.' If he continues, say firmly with a mean look, 'Stop! No! I don't like that!' Then, if he still doesn't stop, get an adult to help." I stressed the importance of matching the verbal and nonverbal cues. "Nicely" requires a pleasant-looking face and a gentle voice. "Firmly" requires a not-so-nice face with a louder, lower voice.

Then we role-played:

NATE. Hey, you, why do you always wear a red shirt? Every day you wear it. That's dumb.

KENNY. Nate, please stop. I don't like it when you talk to me like that.

NATE. Well, change your shirt then, so I don't have to say it.

KENNY. Stop. No. I don't like that.

NATE. Kenny always wears that, Kenny always wears that.

KENNY. Ms. Candy, I've asked Nate twice to stop teasing me. I told him I don't like it, but he won't listen.

As silly as it sounds, this role-playing worked like a charm. It validated my charge. He now knew his feelings were justified: it isn't fun when someone teases you. It empowered him with practical ways to deal with the situation. He was given skills to solve the problem on his own. He was also given a backup plan if his initial solution didn't

Nanny Tip

Here are a few conversation starters that you can teach your child:

- "That looks like fun. Can I join in?"
- "Can you show me how to play that game [do that activity, etc.]?"
- "What's your name? I'm Sam."
- "Hey there, can I play with you guys?"
- "Got room for an extra person?"

resolve the issue. The next time he was teased, he was so proud of himself because his solution worked. It built his confidence and self-esteem because he now knew that he could gain the respect of his peers by clearly communicating his feelings and asking that the offending behavior stop. He was in control of the situation and no longer had to accept the unwanted behavior.

This is also a time when as a parent you may be hearing a lot of "I have no friends, nobody likes me, and no one plays with me." You may also often hear, "Robbie was my best friend—how could he do that?" Be sensitive. This is your child's perception, and for the time being, this is more important than what is happening in actuality.

Ask open-ended questions like, "What makes you feel this way?" to try to discover the root of the perception. If he says, "No one plays with me," teach him how to ask if he can join in. If someone has hurt his feelings, teach him to express what is going through his head to the offender. Set up some successful playdates with the friends he does have, to rebuild his self-esteem and to give him practice "playing." Role-play with family members (for older kids) or even stuffed animals and dolls (for younger ones), and encourage him to take initiative in making friends.

Sports and Style

Even as young as age six, boys with solid sports skills and girls with a taste for fashion are looked up to by their classmates and find peer acceptance quite natural.

Trust me, I've seen it. One of my charges is a natural-born athlete—the kind you'd think was born with a baseball in his hand. By first grade, he was the organizer of recess sports games that often included older kids, and he had no problem jumping into a neighborhood game of pickup basketball with kids twice his age and size. No one questioned him, because he could play. He was six years old, but age was no object to him. If the kids had tried to have a conversation with him beforehand, the age difference would have been apparent, and I doubt he would have been invited to play. But this young guy had confidence in himself and his ability and knew how to integrate himself into a group. He'd just saunter up to any group playing ball and say, "Need another player?" and he was in.

By age ten, the "in crowd" is in full formation. The boys who are great at sports and the girls who dress the most fashionably have become the cool kids—the ones all the other kids want to be around. They are the popular kids, the ones who are never left out.

The older the children get, the more outward appearance and skill play a role in the social success of a child. It is sad but true. Suddenly the boy who was labeled as the loner is discovered to have a mean fastball. Any social ineptness is now history, and all the boys want him on their team.

It is a time when one new outfit or hairstyle seems to change the entire life of a fifth-grade girl. All of a sudden, everyone wants to know, "Where did you get that?" and they want it too. They want to be around her because they want her sense of style or popularity to rub off on them. They are drawn to outward appearance. This is when old adages like "All that glitters isn't gold" and "You can't judge a book by its cover" begin to take real meaning in a way a child can understand.

When your child suddenly wants to be part of the "in crowd" and is looking to her peers for acceptance, don't panic—hang tight. You haven't lost your influential role. Although it may seem like your child is ignoring your thoughts and opinions about life, remember that almost all polls show that kids rate their parents as their number one heroes. But they are trying to survive on School Island without getting voted off the playground, and at times their desperation to climb to the top of the social hill (no matter who they step on to get there) is palpable.

> *The best way to destroy an enemy is to make him a friend.*
> —Abraham Lincoln

Although the "what's cool to wear" and "how to style their hair" influence may come from their peers, guidance on the inner qualities of your children's morals and values will still come from you.

Mean Behavior in Good Kids

I often say that all kids are good—it's their behavior that sometimes stinks. I really believe that. So do my charges. The other day, Austin and his mom were role-playing about making new friends at a new school, and Austin practiced introducing himself to a friend on the playground. He began by saying, "Hi, I'm Austin. I am a good kid who sometimes does bad behavior." We got a good laugh, but we took great comfort in knowing that he knows the true score: he is a great kid who sometimes flubs up. (Aren't we all?)

Unfortunately, your child will be in an environment where, at times, the bad behavior of a child will significantly outweigh the good. They will be in an environment where some children present have never heard of the Golden Rule, or if they have, they believe it means, "He who has the gold, rules." Of course, the majority of classmates will be socially versed in classroom kindness, but occasionally you'll run into one whose compassion skills are lagging behind.

> ### *Nanny Tip*
>
> Always address the behavior, not the child. "Those words are hurtful" is much more effective than "You are so mean." Children are all good, but their behavior sometimes stinks.

This is a sad situation, because most of the mean behavior—gossip, teasing, bullying—is most likely learned behavior, or at least behavior that should have been identified and nipped in the bud long before grade school. That said, although the bad behavior of the child is unacceptable, as parents and caregivers, we need to be sensitive to the whole picture—one that was not painted overnight.

Most elementary-school kids who display mean behavior do so because they haven't quite figured out how to fit in. They are calling out for attention. They are trying to find their place in the miniature world of the classroom. If a child loves attention, even the negative sort, then he realizes fairly quickly that kids and teachers will give him plenty of attention when he calls another student a bad name. The whole class is riveted on the drama unfolding around him! He wants to be part of the group but hasn't yet grasped the other, more successful options available to him.

Sometimes a child behaves in these ways because he is imitating what he has observed at home by an older sibling or a parent. Sometimes it's because he is trying to protect himself from being hurt by others. He's learned that if he does the hurting first, he is in control. ("I'll push you away before you push me away.") Sometimes it's because he has pent-up emotions and hasn't been given a proper outlet to release them.

Nanny Tip

The following model can help your child develop a healthy pattern of problem solving:

- What is the problem? Determine what the conflict is.
- Who is involved? Determine who is involved and what role they play in the conflict.
- Is it a necessary or unnecessary conflict? Is it a mean comment that can be ignored, or is it worth taking the time to invest in coming to a solution?
- What does each party feel? Listen respectfully to the opinions and desires of all involved.
- Brainstorm solutions. Evaluate the pros and cons of the solutions that come up. Is there a win-win situation? What are the pros and cons of each possible solution?
- Choose a solution and stick to it. Agree to the solution that has the most potential for a win-win outcome.
- Evaluate how the solution is working. If it is not working, try another.

If your child seems to be the one with mean behavior, take time to talk with the teacher to find out what is going on in school. Address the behaviors and come up with a plan to curb them. Evaluate what is going on at home. How does your child perceive his place in the family? Does he feel like he fits in? Review the social strategies above. A child who has good social skills will have friends. Make time to practice and role-play interacting with other children. If you give your child an alternative, positive way to get attention or to fit in, he may just choose it.

If your child is on the receiving end of the mean behavior, take time to listen to how he is feeling. Talk through ways of dealing with a child who teases him, and teach him the importance of conflict resolution.

Conflict Resolution

Wouldn't it be great if conflicts never happened? Unfortunately, life seems to guarantee them. That said, it is important, from a young age, to teach children to resolve conflicts they will face in a productive, healthy manner rather than trying to avoid conflict at all costs.

What a delight it is to make friends with someone you have despised!
—Anonymous

The Bible says, "Blessed are the peace*makers*," not the "peace*keepers*."[1] There is a difference between being proactive in making peace and being a doormat who allows himself to be walked on to keep the peace.

Kids will get teased; kids will encounter behaviors that they wish would stop. Through conflict resolution, children learn real-life skills they will need to be successful. If children are taught how to resolve conflicts peacefully and successfully, they will learn how to express their opinions, listen to others' opinions, respect ideas that differ from theirs, and come up with win-win solutions through negotiating. They will also learn to gracefully accept win-lose situations and the occasional situations in which people have to agree to disagree.

Inevitably, there will be times when your child needs to accept defeat with honor, especially on the sports field. How can you teach a child to lose gracefully? You teach her to acknowledge that for some reason—maybe it's better skill, maybe it's more experience, maybe it's pure luck—today just wasn't her day to win. You nonchalantly approach the topic with, "Sometimes you win, and sometimes you lose." You encourage your child always to do her best and always to demand good sportsmanship. When she is defeated, teach her to congratulate her opponent. When she's the defeater, teach her to praise the others' efforts and to thank them for playing.

> ### *Nanny Tip*
>
> Help your child have patience with kids of different personality types by pointing out strengths in others when your child may only see an area of weakness. For example, you might say, "Yes, I see that Joe may be loud and bossy sometimes, but he is a really great leader and has been a loyal friend to you."

The Parental Pause

As a nanny (and lover of control), I have experienced times when I have desperately wanted to solve my charges' problems for them—right then, right there. One day when he was in first grade, Fraser came out of school crying. I asked him, "What's the matter?" He told me that his friend had just bit him! I was livid. The boy, whom I knew quite well, was standing next to Fraser, and I was ready to give it to him good, complete with the nanny "evil eye," but I decided it was better for the teacher and boys to handle it since it happened during school. (Good thing for the friend!)

I took a deep breath, calmly escorted Fraser to the teacher, and said, "Fraser needs to talk to you." I stepped away and let the student and teacher chat about what had happened. The teacher comforted Fraser and then got the other student, sat them both down, kneeled to their level, and began resolving the problem. A few minutes later, the friend apologized and issued a well-received hug. Fraser accepted his apology, and they were ready to play together that afternoon. Fraser was dismissed, and the friend and his mom entered the school for a brief meeting with the teacher.

The kids made up, and all was well. I was thrilled at how the teacher handled the situation. He addressed the problem, guided the communication of the children, had them suggest solutions, and then followed up with the offender's parent. Beautiful! I couldn't have done it better—but the teacher had an advantage: no emotional attachments.

I was still unhappy over the incident and didn't want Fraser anywhere near the kid (at least for the rest of that day). But they went on like nothing had happened, and for the sake of their friendship, I decided to follow their lead.

I remember that when I first became a nanny, my mom warned me never to get involved with the kids' arguments unless there was blood. (OK, that's a bit of an exaggeration, but you get the point.) "Long after the children resolve and forget the issue," she taught me, "the parents (and nanny) still carry the emotional upset and hold on to the momentary scars that no longer exist on the child's body or in their minds." Mom was right.

So what I have learned, I will offer to you. Whenever possible, let kids work things out on their own. No matter how tempting, try not to jump in too soon. Let them try to resolve it by themselves, with a distant, watchful eye from you. Most likely, they are going to make up and forgive and forget quickly; and if we get involved, we are left to hold on to grudges that don't even belong to us.

Teach Your Kids About Personality Types

In their award-winning book *The Two Sides of Love*, Gary Smalley and John Trent describe the four basic personality types in ways that even children can understand, by using animals as examples:

- *Lions* are born leaders, but their "Follow me!" roars can sometimes be abrasive, if not tamed.
- *Otters* are playful and outgoing, encouraging and likable, but organization is often not their strong suit.
- *Golden retrievers* are laid-back and loyal, but they can be overly passive in their efforts to please everyone.
- *Beavers* are nose-to-the-grindstone workers who accomplish tasks with streamlined efficiency but can forget to take breaks and enjoy relationships.[2]

Of course, most people have a combination of two or more of these personality types, but usually one is so dominant that we laughingly, and almost instantly, recognize ourselves and one another in these animals.

When you teach your children about the various personalities and the positive and negative traits of each one, they can become more educated and empathetic in their interactions with others. Observe other people in the family and kids they know, and ask your child, "Do you think Mike is more of a beaver or an otter or a lion or a golden retriever? Or maybe a combination of two of them? What do you think is the best way to approach a lion? How can you help a beaver get his head out of the books and go outside to play?"

Talking about these things will deepen your child's intuition about others, help him develop people skills to last a lifetime, and hopefully ward off some unanticipated "lion" attack. I highly recommend this book to parents, kids, educators, and, of course, nannies!

 ### Scene 7: Take 2
On the Playground

JARED. Let's play keep-away from Kevin!
KEVIN. Why do I always have to be in the middle? It's no fun.

JARED. Come on, knucklehead. It's because you never get the ball and the game lasts long!

KEVIN. That's not fair, Jared, and you know it. I like to play, and I don't mind having my turn in the middle, but let's trade off.

JARED. Kevin, we *let* you play! Isn't that cool! Look at Jimmy. We don't let him play.

KEVIN. Well, I'll find someone else to be in the middle if you can't play fair. I don't like how you are treating me—or Jimmy. (*He walks over to Jimmy to see what he is doing. The two of them find a third player and in no time are enjoying a game of keep-away where each one takes a turn in a different position.*)

Nanny to the Rescue Again! Recap

What techniques did Kevin use to put an end to the unfair treatment?

1. *He identified his feelings.* He didn't like the way he was being treated. It didn't feel good.

2. *He expressed his feelings to the offender.* "That's not fair, and you know it."

3. *He offered a suggestion to the problem.* "Let's play fair."

4. *When his suggestion wasn't accepted and the offending behavior continued, he walked away.* He valued himself enough to know that he didn't have to accept treatment that hurt him.

5. *He showed empathy for another child.* When he realized another kid was also being treated unfairly, he made an effort to reach out.

6. *He demonstrated leadership.* He initiated a new game, where fair play would reign.

CHAPTER EIGHT

FRIENDSHIP FACTORS

 Scene 8: Take 1
The Neighborhood Front Yard

CAROLYN, *walking outside in her front yard, spying her friend Darla.* Hey, Darla, want to play badminton? We just got a new net up in the backyard.

DARLA. Sure, but here comes Alicia, and she'll want to play too.

CAROLYN. Oh nooo . . .

ALICIA. Hey! What are you two up to? Want to play a game?

CAROLYN. Sorry, two is company, but three's a crowd.

DARLA. Can't three play badminton?

CAROLYN. I guess they could, but not at my house. Besides, I only have two rackets.

(Alicia walks slowly back into her house, feeling understandably rejected.)

ALICIA'S MOM. Honey, what's the matter?

ALICIA. Everyone hates me!

Nobody likes me, everybody hates me, guess I'll go eat worms." Most of us probably vaguely remember singing that song as a child, or at least relating to the lyrics at one time or another. But as a parent or caregiver, hearing them sung by your child is a whole different experience—second verse, same as the first, but a little bit louder and a whole lot worse.

Let's be honest. Even as adults we all occasionally have our own "nobody likes me" pity parties. For example, after a recent surgery, I expected some friends to come visit, but something else came up for all of them at the same time. They did nothing wrong; in fact, they had been an amazing help to me all week. But because I was feeling vulnerable, achy, and not so great about myself, I basically cried the day away. It was a full-fledged tear fest.

A true friend is one who overlooks your failures and tolerates your success!
—Doug Larson

The next morning, the sun came up, and so did my spirits—the pity party was over. After getting some much-needed rest, I was out of bed, making some breakfast and feeling much better. I reminded myself that I have great family and wonderful friends who have been there for me every step of the way. I was back to my normal self.

I bounced back relatively quickly as I confronted my own self-sabotaging thoughts with no basis in truth. But I'm a grown woman. Imagine how hard it is for a child whose emotions aren't yet mature and who can't see past her circumstances to her true value.

What about being left out in a game by a classmate at recess? Sitting by yourself at lunch because you are "the new kid" and haven't found friends yet? Finding out you are the only girl who hasn't been invited to a party? Or being stood up by a friend who promised to come play after school?

As we know, situations like these can hurt a child's feelings so much that she has trouble focusing on school the rest of the day. Even the simplest, most innocent actions of a friend sitting by another girl at lunchtime can sting, especially if your daughter is already having a difficult day. In the world of schoolchildren, lunchtime, free time, and gym class can be some of the toughest times in a child's emotional life. (Unless you were the most popular boy or girl in your class, you probably remember how scary these times could be. What if no one sat with you at lunch? What if you were the dreaded last one picked for softball teams in PE class?)

Because social life among grade-schoolers can be so tough, it is imperative that they have a soft place to land when they come home. Throughout this book, I've emphasized that one of the most important things you can do for your children is to build their self-esteem by loving them for who they are in words and deeds. How? By acknowledging their achievements and helping them through their setbacks; by embracing their individuality and encouraging them always to do their best; by allowing them to take risks, ready to cheer them on and catch them if they fall. A school bully can take a child's lunch, but if a child is confident in who she is at home, at the end of the day her self-esteem is intact.

I'm not saying that your child will never have a bad day or that she will never make a negative comment about herself or will never be hurt by what a classmate says. What I am saying, however, is that if your child is being raised in a loving,

Nanny Tip

Teach your child this valuable lesson: We aren't responsible for making other people happy, nor are we responsible for making them sad. We are only responsible to be kind, polite, and truthful.

Sometimes, no matter how courteously you say something, it's just not what the person wants to hear. For example, you can say to a friend, "I'm sorry I can't go to your house today," in a kind, direct, and polite manner. But the friend may still be upset, sad, or even angry. Your child can validate the friend's feelings: "I'm sorry you feel sad. Maybe we can play tomorrow." Help your child not to take on guilt that isn't his burden to bear.

nurturing environment, where she knows her worth, the hurts will only be momentary setbacks—little bumps in the road rather than gaping potholes.

For the most part, children who are secure in who they are will navigate the schoolyard just fine. If, however, your child truly seems to be in perpetual misery, and all other methods of helping him through his school days are not working, more drastic measures may need to be taken, even putting your child in another school. Sometimes a child gets a label in one particular environment and simply cannot shake it off. Moving to a new school that gives him a fresh start and new surroundings may be one answer, but it should be a last resort.

Friendship Is a Verb

One of my favorite movies is *Anne of Green Gables*, where the impulsive but earnest Anne is on the constant lookout for a true soul mate, a "kindred spirit." As she grows up, she realizes that kindred spirits aren't as scarce as she once thought. The truth is, Anne had grown in her ability to befriend a variety of personality types. To be a friend, according to the wise King Solomon, one must "show himself friendly."[1]

One of the best life lessons you can teach your child is how to be a good friend to others. As you know from life experience, starting, building, and maintaining a friendship takes effort, along with some trial and error.

Depending on your child's temperament, being a good friend may or may not come naturally. For most kids, developing friendships is, at least in part, a learned skill. So for your child to survive the waves of friendship, you'll need to teach him how to build and maintain friendships. Let's look now at some of the qualities that make a good friend.

Good friends are good listeners. Teach your child to listen actively. Encourage him to look a person in the eye and acknowledge or comment on what the other person just said, rather than racing ahead with his own agenda. Show your child how to use good body language to show that he is really listening to, not just hearing, another.

Good friends build one another up and don't tear one another down. Teach your child to encourage, not discourage. Friends don't make fun of one another's weaknesses; they offer help and praise one another's strengths. Even good-natured joking and teasing have to be done very carefully and only among good friends, where both end up laughing together. This will take a little observation and guidance. A good rule of thumb is to not tease anyone—even in a friendly way—unless you really know them well and they know that you really, sincerely like them.

Be kind and compassionate to one another, forgiving each other, just as in Christ God forgave you.
—Ephesians 4:32

Good friends are honest, even when being honest is hard. Teach your child that it is better to be honest than to lie. If they have to tell the truth, and they think it might hurt a friend's feelings, they should do it in a private setting, sitting the friend down and sharing their thoughts as kindly as possible. Teach your child the "sandwich technique"—always sandwich any criticism between two praises.

Good friends are sympathetic and empathetic toward one another. Teach your child to read her friends' facial expressions, how they speak and look, not just what they say. If a friend looks sad, encourage your child to ask if the friend is OK and then lend a listening and concerned ear.

Good friends help one another. Teach your child to be a cheerful giver and grateful receiver. Teach him to give help by offering services, time, or support to a friend. Teach him the importance of accepting help from friends when it is offered.

Good friends give one another the benefit of the doubt. Teach your child to think positively and not to take offense easily. Some children are supersensitive and need to learn to take comments at face value, not reading into them any hidden hostilities. Encourage your child to give others grace for miscommunications, misunderstandings, and mistakes.

Good friends trust one another. Teaching your child the value of trust is essential. When someone tells your child a secret—unless someone will get hurt, is in danger, or needs help—he needs to learn the value of keeping his word. Does everyone at the lunch table really need to know that Gina has a crush on David? Talk through some scenarios so that your child knows when it is important to keep a friend's secret and when keeping a secret could be a bad idea.

Good friends care about one another. Teach your child to be a caring person by expressing in words and in deeds her commitment to a friendship. A smile across

Eight Friendship Breakers

1. *Gossiping.* If you don't have something nice to say, don't say anything, especially behind someone's back. Rumor spreading falls under this category.

2. *Lying.* One lie is all it takes to destroy the trust that has been built up over time. Is it worth it?

3. *Using.* Be friends with someone for who they are, not what they have or what they will give you. Examine your motives.

4. *Betraying.* Don't say one thing and do another. Mean what you say, and say what you mean.

5. *Controlling.* Friends don't try to control one another or tell others what to do.

6. *Judging.* Accept your friends for who they are. Their personality or ways may be different than yours—it doesn't always mean that they are right or wrong.

7. *Constantly competing.* Friends don't need to constantly compete. Encourage your friends' strengths and help them improve their weaknesses.

8. *Promise breaking.* Don't make a promise that you can't keep or don't plan to keep.

the room to a friend who is down in the dumps could brighten her day. There's nothing like the encouragement of a good friend when a child is feeling blue. Help your child know the power of a positive word given freely to others.

Good friends are dependable. Teach your child to keep commitments. Make sure your child knows that it is not OK to change plans with a friend because "a better offer" came up.

Good friends understand that people change—and love them anyway. Teach your child that people grow and change, and we need to love them for who they are because we grow and change too. There are three kinds of friends: friends you have for a reason (teammates, neighborhood playmates, those who go to the same church), friends you have for a season of time that ends, and friends you have for a lifetime.

Good friends love one another even through tough times. Teach your child that friendships aren't always perfect, but when arguments and disagreements arise, true friends will, in the end, work them out.

Nanny Tip

In our Christian Nannies group, we have a tradition of anonymously sending notes, small tokens, homemade goodies, or other inexpensive, thoughtful gifts to other nannies in the group. These anonymous gifts have brightened the hearts of many people. You can help your child learn the joy of giving by choosing a "secret blessing" tradition in your own family once a week or once a month.

Not Everyone Will Like You All of the Time

Let's say that you've taught your child the keys to friendship building. She is confident that she knows how to be a good friend. But there is one girl at school who doesn't like her. Maybe even two or three. She can't figure out why. Now what?

Here's a reality check: no matter what you do or how nice you are, there are going to be people in this world who for some reason simply won't like you. One child therapist calls it the 80-20 rule of friendship. Most people will like you, but about 20 percent of them won't—and there's not a thing you can do about it but let it roll off your emotions like water off a duck's back. Sad as it seems, it is one of those odd facts of life for everyone. For people-pleaser types, this is a hard truth. But understanding this principle will help to free your child's mind from endless ping-ponging—trying to figure out why another child doesn't like her, ruminating endlessly on what she can do to persuade her to change her mind. (In fact, this can be a very freeing truth for grown-ups to accept!)

Another safeguard for your children is to encourage them to have several friends. Now, they don't all have to be best, best friends (that "kindred spirit" we all hope to find and treasure). But if you have a variety of friends, you'll soon find out that you don't need a one-size-fits-all friend who fits every occasion. Justin may not be much fun to play chess with, but he's great for going on bike rides. Lisa is a blast to go to the movies with, but she may not like just hanging out and chatting. That's OK. Enjoy what each friend can bring to your life, and don't stew over their imperfections or flaws.

When your child experiences her first friendship rejection, be ready to listen to her share her concerns and disappointments. (I recommend keeping a box of Kleenex nearby.) Encourage her to focus not on the friends she doesn't have but on the blessing of the ones she does have. Maybe the friend who's rebuffing your daughter is the popular girl. If this seems to be the case, you might say, "Tell me about Stacie. Why do you like her?" Maybe it's not that your daughter really wants Stacie to be her friend so badly, but it is the act of rejection that hurts. (And granted, rejection is one of the most painful of human emotions.) Help her see that sometimes we want a friend for the status symbol she might give us, such as hanging out with the popular girl, hoping her popularity will rub off on us. But if the same girl wasn't popular, would you want to spend time with her, just for fun?

Acknowledge that your child won't like everyone all of the time, nor does she have to befriend her entire class. Even so, there's no excuse for being mean or rude to children who are simply not your child's cup of tea. We can all be respectful and kind for short periods of time, even if another person's personality grates us like fingernails scraping a chalkboard. Don't try to force friendships on behalf of your child—they will happen naturally. Or not.

Handling Momentary Defeats

The rejection has taken place; the attempt at a friendship has failed. Whether your child got rejected or the other way around, this is a good time to teach your child about showing grace and caring for feelings. "Even if you don't like someone," you might say, "they have feelings too. It is OK and natural for there to be some kids you don't like or who don't like you. Just try to remember how you felt when you were on the other side, and apply that Golden Rule we've been talking about."

When your child is approached by a classmate he just doesn't click with, how should he handle the situation? You should encourage him not to gossip or speak poorly about the other child. And you should also encourage him not to alienate the classmate, especially if the boy isn't doing anything wrong—it's just that their personalities don't mesh. For short periods of time, we can all be polite to people we don't particularly like. It's part of life's little realities, part of growing up.

When to Intervene, When to Wait It Out

When your child has experienced rejection by a friend, this is a vital time for you, as a parent, to develop and exercise some

Nanny Tip

Remember, your children are watching to see if you do what you say. Be a good role model in the area of personal relationships. The next time you want to get someone back or make a rude comment after feeling slighted, remember that your children are watching.

new skills of your own. It is hard to see your child hurting or feeling blue. It is painful to see her eyes well up with tears. Every bone in your parental body wants to jump in immediately and fix it, to take the pain away. My knee-jerk impulse is to say to myself, "That kid is rotten. How could he do that to my precious boy?"

But this is the time to hold your tongue and stay calm. Keep in mind that at this young age, twenty-four hours can change worst enemies to friends and best friends to worst enemies. Childhood friendships are built, broken, and rebuilt in the blink of an eye.

The Perks of Taking the High Road

Fraser, my first-grade charge, recently came home from school with a story about kindness over rejection. "Shell, the girl who sits next to me, Katie, asked me my favorite colors. I told her yellow and orange. She then took out a yellow and an orange marker and wrote in her school journal, 'I hate Fraser.'"

My heart sank, and my eyes began to well up in empathy. Then he told me the kicker. "But, Shell, you'll be proud. I wrote in my journal, 'Katie hates me but I like her anyway.'" I went from sad tears to tears of pride. He was sincere and seemed pleased with his choice not to let her hurtful actions affect his self-esteem or his decision to be kind. He made the choice to take the high road.

As Eleanor Roosevelt said, "No one can make you feel inferior without your permission." Fraser refused to give Katie permission, and his response turned a momentary slight into a moment of inner victory.

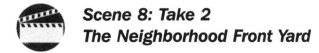

Scene 8: Take 2
The Neighborhood Front Yard

CAROLYN, *walking outside in her front yard, spying her friend Darla.* Hey, Darla, want to play badminton? We just got a new net up in the backyard.

DARLA. Sure, but here comes Alicia, and she'll want to play too.

CAROLYN. Oh nooo . . .

ALICIA. Hey! What are you two up to? Want to play a game?

CAROLYN. Sorry, two is company, but three's a crowd.

DARLA. Can't three play badminton?

CAROLYN. I guess they could, but not at my house. Besides, I only have two rackets.

ALICIA. Well, I have a couple of rackets at home, and we could all play. Or I could go get my sister, Karla, and see if she wants to join us so we could play with even teams.

DARLA. That's a great idea. It'd be a lot more fun with more, right, Carolyn?

(Carolyn nods, knowing she's outnumbered and giving in to Darla's kinder impulses.)

(Alicia smiles gratefully at Darla and goes to get her sister and the rackets. The four of them end up having a fabulous time, and even Carolyn begins to realize how much more fun it is to play badminton with four rather than two.)

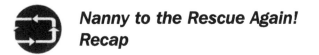

Nanny to the Rescue Again!
Recap

How did Alicia adjust to Carolyn's initial rejecting statement?

1. *She ignored Carolyn's bad attitude.* She didn't call attention to Carolyn but rather focused on solving the situation.

2. *She offered an alternative.* She said that her friends could play at her house, or she could bring extra rackets to Carolyn's house.

3. *She helped even up the numbers by suggesting she bring along her sister as a teammate.* Odd numbers, especially three, tend to force sides. Kids usually play better in even numbers.

4. *She connected with Darla, the girl who was friendlier and kinder.* This overtook the more selfish Carolyn without excluding her.

5. *Alicia never let Carolyn "see her sweat" with insecurity.* She kept her head high and got creative instead.

CHAPTER NINE

TAKING A BITE OUT OF BULLYING

 ### Scene 9: Take 1
In the Cafeteria

JAMIE. Hey, Sarah. Did you hear that Rachel is afraid of the dark and won't sleep with the lights out?

SARAH. Jamie, you *have* to be kidding. Rachel is such a baby.

NATALIE. I know—I can't believe it.

JAMIE, *motioning from the table across the room.* Hey, Rachel, come sit with us. We're planning a sleepover party.

RACHEL, *walking over to the table.* Sure.

JAMIE. Do you want to come? Oh, I forgot. Only girls who can sleep in the dark are invited. No babies allowed.

SARAH, *sing-songing loudly enough for the whole table to hear.* Rachel-baby sucks her thumb, wipes her face with bubble gum . . . and has to have her nighty-night light on.

JAMIE. Hey, where's your diaper bag, Rachel-baby?

(Rachel turns and walks away, head down, tears falling, looking for a place to escape from her tormenters.)

According to *Webster's Dictionary*, bullying is "treating one in an overbearing or intimidating manner." It takes on many forms, including name-calling, intimidation, intentional embarrassment, and harassment. It can be verbal or physical, emotional or psychological. It is, in short, a real form of child abuse—but it usually happens on a peer-to-peer level. Like other forms of abuse, there is a victim and there is an abuser. It may consist of one child bullying another, or it may consist of a group of kids singling out one child.

Bullying goes beyond the everyday childhood squabbles and hurt feelings of playground politics. It even goes beyond the occasional playground riff between two classmates. The line between squabbles and bullying can be clearly drawn when there is a repeated, conscious effort on the part of one child to control another child, usually one who appears to be weaker or smaller than average or seems to be different in some way. Low self-esteem (masked as domination), skewed thinking patterns, and basic lack of respect for others is at the core of bully behavior, at any age and stage.

Our children say bullying and teasing are a big problem. In a 2001 survey conducted by the Kaiser Family Foundation and Nickelodeon, "Talking with Kids About Tough Issues," 74 percent of the eight- to eleven-year-olds surveyed said that teasing and bullying occur at their school. Of the twelve- to fifteen-year-olds, 86 percent said that bullying and teasing occur at their school.[1] The problem is all too common.

Who Bullies?

Sadly, bullying behavior is often a learned response, and the kids learn it from—you guessed!—interactions at home. There are exceptions, such as children who have genetic emotional or mental disorders, but as a general rule, kids who bully are simply mimicking what they've seen, or they are operating by a survival instinct due to parental neglect.

As *Reader's Digest* reports, "Researchers, led by Kris Bosworth of the University of Arizona, collected information from 558 students in grades 6 to 8, then divided the students into three groups: 228 who rarely or never bullied anyone; 243 who reported a moderate level of bullying; and 87 who reported excessive amounts of bullying. Those who reported the most bullying behavior had received more forceful, physical discipline from their parents, had viewed more TV violence and showed more misconduct at home. Thirty-two percent lived with a stepparent, and 36 percent lived in a single-parent household. Bullies generally had fewer adult role models, more exposure to gang activity, and easier access to guns. This partly explains why bullies need help as much as victims: Many learn their behavior by example."[2]

Children who bully often do so to

According to the Coalition for Children Safe Kids campaign, children who are targeted by bullies tend to have the following traits in common:

• low self-esteem
• insecure
• lack of social skills
• don't pick up on social cues
• cry or become emotionally distraught easily
• unable to defend or stand up for themselves

Children who are confident and know that they are valued by those closest to them are less likely to be the victims of bullying.

try to gain status among their peers. They often haven't learned the social skills to make friends, so by force and fear they find their role among their classmates. Bullying gives a sense of power to children who often feel powerless in their own lives—ones who are dealing with overwhelming situations that are out of their control. By pushing others around, they can exercise the control that is lacking in their own family or school lives.

I shared with you in previous chapters some tips on helping your child build self-esteem, learn communication skills, and manage conflicts with peers. Your child will be a confident and empowered young person if he or she has the tools to deal with the constant ups and downs of grade-school life.

Bullies Happen—on Mars and Venus

It's a common misconception that only boys bully and are the victims of bullies. The reality is that both boys and girls experience bullying; it just manifests itself in different forms.

Boys usually inflict physical or verbal pain on their victims. They may push and shove and take part in loud name-calling. They are blunt and enjoy the attention of bullying in front of their peers. Boys usually stick to bullying other boys, but occasionally they will also bully girls. This is usually in the form of making derogatory or sexual comments.

Girls are subtler and will usually inflict emotional or psychological pain on their victims. They are more likely to exclude their victim from the lunch table or spread rumors about her than to trip a peer on the playground. They will ignore a classmate and ensure that she knows that she was selectively not invited to a birthday party or sleepover. Girls usually stick to bullying other girls, but they can be very influential in getting others to jump on their bullying bandwagon.

How to Know if Your Child Is Being Bullied

Of course, there are obvious telltale signs that something isn't going right with your child at school. Bumps, bruises, and ripped clothing are outright indicators that there is reason for concern.

There are also less obvious clues that something isn't right, and to pick up on them, you really need to be in tune with the reality that bullying occurs more frequently then you may think. Perhaps your child is experiencing generalized unexplained anxiety or has missing schoolwork or books, or maybe there is a sudden change in your child's sleeping or eating patterns or new mysterious excuses for not wanting to attend school. These subtle shifts in behavior shouldn't be ignored. Ask questions like, "What is it like on the school playground?" "Are any kids picked on at school?" "What goes on at lunchtime?" These are all questions that give a nonconfrontational opportunity for your child to share his thoughts and concerns.

How do you teach a child to handle bullying? One encouraging report shows that children are generally pretty attuned to how to handle bullies effectively. In 1999, the directors of the Maine Project Against Bullying requested that the Center for Educational Policy, Applied Research, and Evaluation at the University of Southern Maine analyze the survey results of 4,496 third-grade students in the state of Maine. This study resulted in a technical report entitled "A Survey of Bullying Behavior Among Maine Third Graders." The study found that "in response to bullying acts, almost all (91.3%) of third graders take some action: almost one-half tell an adult, followed by one-third (34.2%) who tell the bully to stop and who get away from the bully (32%). Although a very small percentage (2.1%), some children, when confronted with bullying, will hurt others. Finally, one-half of children perceive that the result of their having reported bullying is an improvement of the situation."[3]

Nanny Tip

Open-ended questions usually lead to lots more interesting information. Asking, "Did you have a good day?" will get you a one-word response, while asking, "Tell me about your day," encourages a more spontaneous and creative response.

Teach Your Child How to Deal with a Bully

What should you do when you find out that your child is being bullied? First, you need to objectively evaluate the situation. Yes, this is easier said than done, but what your child needs right now is a good listener rather than an angry parent. If you convey anger to your child, he may misconstrue your response as disappointment, or he may fear that you may take action, which he would perceive as causing more problems than he has already endured.

> ### Nanny Tip
>
> When a bully knows his victim has friends who will stick up for him, he's likely to back off. A simple "Hey, he's my friend. Knock it off!" could stop a situation or at least prevent it from escalating long enough to find a teacher to help.

Your child also needs you to validate his feelings, but be sure you do so with a nonjudgmental attitude until you have all the facts. Don't place blame on anyone, but assure your child that you are listening and hearing how he is feeling and that you absolutely agree that it is no fun to experience what he perceives as happening. Assure him that there is a win-win solution to the problem and that together you'll come up with a plan.

Give your child tips on how to deal with the bully. There are several schools of thought on how to handle a bully, ranging from fighting back to walking away. When my charges have been put in a bullying situation, I have taught them the following tips on dealing with the situation:

Avoid the bully. Avoid unsupervised areas where the bully knows he won't get caught, and try to use the buddy system for extra support.

Have clear, strong body language. Stand up straight and look the bully in the eyes. If you are scared, don't show it.

Say, "Stop! No! I don't like that!" Make sure you say these words with a glaring look and a firm voice. If the bully doesn't stop, walk away.

Use humor. If the bully calls you "four eyes," respond calmly with, "Four are better than two." Sometimes humor will throw the bully off, because he will see that you were not bothered and won't know how to respond.

Tell an adult. Let a teacher know what is going on. Remind your child it is never tattling if someone is at risk of getting hurt.

If the bullying continues, and no adult is around, I tell my charges never to throw the first punch, but not to allow themselves to get beat up either. "Your words are always your first form of defense, but be sure to defend yourself physically if the need arises." I have seen a bully silenced the first time some brave kid was willing to call his bluff. As a youngster, I recall seeing a child get spit on day after day; then the first time the child spit back at the bully, the problem ended then and there.

As with any parenting advice, take what applies to you and your family, and leave the rest. Some bullying situations are obviously more dangerous than others, and intervention by an adult is a must. Some may not agree with this advice, but it has worked for me and the families I have served.

What Should You Do When Your Child Is Bullied?

Now you have some insight into how to identify if your child is being bullied, and you have some basic guidelines on how to advise your child if he is getting bullied. But as the parent of a victimized child, what should you do?

Believe your child. Don't accuse him of being too sensitive or having thin skin.

Don't blame your child. Stay away from "If you only did this" statements that can shift the responsibility of the incident to the victim.

Build up your child's self-esteem. Remind him what he is good at, and help him get involved with activities that promote growth in those areas.

 Nanny Tip

Children love hearing stories from your childhood. Sharing your elementary-school memories often opens up a dialogue about a topic your child might naturally shy away from discussing. Take a moment to jot down some childhood memories, particularly those that have an encouraging or empathetic angle to them. Share them at appropriate times.

Role-play with your child. Act out situations that teach him how to be assertive and firm in expressing himself to the bully.

Don't promise that you won't tell. Be up front with your child that the behavior is unacceptable and needs to stop, and let him know your plan of action.

Get all the facts. Find out the who, what, when, and where, and if there were any witnesses or others who came to his defense.

Talk to your child's teacher about the situation in a calm manner. If she is non-responsive, go to the principal. Most schools have antibullying policies.

Develop a plan of action with the teacher. Follow up with the teacher to make sure the bullying stops.

Do not confront the parents of the bully alone. If the bullying happens in school, treat it as a school issue. Involve a counselor, teacher, or principal to help solve the problem.

Foster other friendships for your child. Have playdates to build a support system of peers for your child.

Unfortunately, the truth is that most children will eventually encounter another child who displays mean behaviors. Since this is the reality, it is important that your child is prepared and has some strategies to deal with the behaviors he will encounter. This is one situation where proactive parenting can prevent permanent injuries of the mind, body, and soul.

When Your Child Is the Bully

I remember the first time I heard that *my* charge was mean to another child. He was three, and he bit another child in a Mommy and Me literacy class we were taking. I think it's a natural, protective reaction to think, *Surely not my child!* Unfortunately, that isn't always the case.

Once you learn that your child is displaying some undesirable behaviors, bordering on bullying, it is important that you immediately address the situation. I have found that conveying a great sense of disappointment is much more effective than showing anger. Every child wants the approval of his parents or caregiver. Communicating disappointment in the behavior of a child has a lasting impact, much longer than the impact of a screaming session. In a calm way, state your feelings: "I am not happy with the choice you made. Hurting people is not something we do. I don't know where you learned this behavior, but it is unacceptable and makes me hurt to see you do it."

For you to say this, it must be true. As we learned above, many children bully because they are imitating what they see. Set a good example for your child. Ironically, it is tempting to react in bullying ways toward a child who is being a bully! Treat the bully in a kind but firm manner, and you will defuse his anger and allow him to redirect his emotions in healthier ways. You will also model for him how to handle a situation that pushes your emotional buttons.

We also learned that often kids bully because they don't feel good about themselves or they are overwhelmed and don't know how to handle situations that are happening in their lives. In a nonconfrontational way, ask some questions to help you find out what your child's pattern of behavior is with other kids.

"What do you enjoy doing with your friends?"

"Tell me about your school life."

"What do you do when someone makes you angry at school?"

If you are able to find out what is causing your child's bullying behavior, try to address it. Is it low self-esteem? Try building him up with purposeful praise. "You are really good at baseball; let's try to get some practice in every night after dinner." If the underlying issue seems to be anger or a short fuse, provide a positive outlet such as a sport or deep-breathing exercises to give him a way to get the stress out of his system. If it's because he is overwhelmed

Nanny Tip

I always enforce a "no-tolerance" bullying policy, so my charges know that if they bully another child, there will be discipline or consequences immediately following. We don't bully. End of story.

with his schoolwork, get him a tutor or talk to the teacher about how you might work as a team to help your child feel more successful and less overwhelmed.

However tempting it may be to avoid the problem, you really need to address it—quickly. If a child learns that bullying behavior is acceptable, he will continue his behavior, possibly into adulthood. According to the KidsHealth for Parents Web site, "As many as one out of four elementary school bullies have a criminal record by the time they're 30."[4]

Putting the Bullying Behavior to Rest

Stopping undesirable behavior won't happen overnight, but there are certainly some methods that can speed up the stopping process.

Be clear that mistreating others is not OK. Point out the unacceptable behavior to the child, and make it clear that it is not OK. "Teasing is unacceptable. We don't do it."

Implement a consequence. Time-outs, loss of privileges, things taken away . . . whatever works, develop a method of discipline and stick to it. Be consistent in the consequences that are imposed for bullying behavior.

Give an opportunity for redemption. Set goals and reward your child when these goals are met. If your child goes one day without calling a classmate a name, give him a sticker. After collecting five stickers, he can earn back a privilege.

Enlist help from the teachers. Work with the teachers on an action plan that can be used both at home and at school.

Set a good example for your child. Teach your child by example how to respect people, their ideas, and their passions. Remind them that different isn't always wrong.

Point out inappropriate behavior when you see it on TV or in public, and explain why it is mean or hurtful behavior. Encourage your children to stick up for others who are being victimized: they can get help from an adult, or they can use positive peer pressure to help curb the actions of the bully.

Teach your child that everyone is valuable and has a purpose. Your child may not like each person he encounters, and every person may not like him, but regardless, we should always treat others the way we want to be treated. Share with him that even as adults, if we are being treated in a way that makes us feel scared or bad, we have every right to get help—and even as a child, so does he.

 ### Scene 9: Take 2
In the Cafeteria

JAMIE. Hey, Sarah. Did you hear that Rachel is afraid of the dark and won't sleep with the lights out?

SARAH. Jamie, you *have* to be kidding. Rachel is such a baby.

NATALIE. I can't believe it, but come on, be nice. We all have things that people could say make us babies.

JAMIE, *motioning from the table across the room.* Hey, Rachel, come sit with us. We're planning a sleepover party.

RACHEL, *walking over to the table.* Sure.

JAMIE. Do you want to come? Oh, I forgot. Only girls who can sleep in the dark are invited. Sorry.

NATALIE. Jamie, that's not too nice a thing to say.

RACHEL. Oh, I guess I can't come then. I like to read at night, so I need the lights on. *(She turns and walks away, head up, to sit with some other friends across the cafeteria.)*

Natalie gets up and follows Rachel.

JAMIE. Oh, I guess maybe I shouldn't have said that. It was kinda mean.

Nanny to the Rescue Again! Recap

What turned this cafeteria cattiness into a confidence-building situation?

1. *The victim used humor.* She acted as if the comment didn't bother her. She gave a smart remark that silenced the bully.

2. *She avoided the bully.* She went across the room and sat with friends, using the buddy system.

3. *Her physical appearance signified strength and confidence.* She didn't have her head down in defeat but held her head up high, showing self-respect.

4. *It only takes one to make a difference.* One girl, Natalie, knew the value of respecting people and wasn't afraid to stand up for her beliefs. Jamie and Sarah were convicted of their behavior once one of their friends showed her disgust.

5. *Positive peer pressure works.* Teach your child not to be afraid to be the leader—most likely, people will follow. One of the girls went over and joined Rachel.

CHAPTER TEN

THE THRILL OF VICTORY AND THE AGONY OF DEFEAT

 Scene 10: Take 1
In the Driveway Playing Basketball

SAM. Come on, you cheated! Mom, Henri is cheating again!

MOM. Henri, was it Sam's turn? Give him the ball back.

HENRI. But I want another shot. I *never* win at this game.

MOM. Fine! One more shot. Then give it to your brother.

SAM. Mom! No fair! He's cheating! It's my turn. Now he got an extra chance!

MOM. Well, you take one, too, Sam. Just work it out.

SAM. Come on, Henri, give me the ball. You aren't playing fair!

HENRI. Mom said I could have another chance.

MOM. Where does it say "referee" in my job description?

'm winning, I'm winning, I'm winning, winning, winning, winning . . . " was Fraser's theme song during his first months of learning to play board games. It got quite frustrating for his twin brother, Austin, who didn't pick up on the strategy of checkers until a bit later. It also got frustrating for me, the unofficial board game coach/referee, listening to the repetitive (and increasingly obnoxious) chorus. But in the end, the one who got most frustrated was Fraser, because Austin no longer wanted to play—and I no longer wanted to coach.

No one wants to play with a sore loser, and no one wants to play with a boastful winner. Granted, when you lose it feels bad, and when you win it feels great. That's the nature of the competitive beast. How do you teach children to enjoy victory and accept defeat with grace (so that they'll continue to have friends who want to play with them)? It is never too early to talk about good sportsmanship, not just in backyard ball or on school teams, but in all of life.

> *Being defeated is often a temporary condition. Giving up is what makes it permanent.*
> —Marilyn vos Savant

You might begin by looking up the word *sportsmanship* together in a dictionary. Here's what I found in *Webster's*: "conduct and attitude considered as befitting participants in sports, especially fair play, courtesy, striving spirit, and grace in losing." Take apart the definition phrase by phrase, and chat with your children about what each word means and how these concepts might apply to their young lives right now. How do you show "fair play" in a board game? Can you think of a way you can show "courtesy" when you play video games? How can you show "grace in losing" when you don't get your way or win the final round of Go Fish?

The elementary-school years are filled with opportunities to take part in new activities: team sports, individual sports, relay races, chess clubs, spelling bees, and playground games like foursquare and kickball. Whether they are formally organized or quick pickup games, these opportunities welcome your child into the competitive world. When the doors open, be prepared to let in all that accompanies competition: the tears over defeat and the joys over victory, the pride when you win and the disappointment when you lose. Anger, frustration, joy, and excitement can all be experienced during a twenty-minute half on the basketball court. What would appear to be a simple game of checkers between friends can hastily end with the board being thrown over, tears shed, and frustrated stomps out of the room. For children who are both sensitive and competitive by nature, losing at anything can be scary, with emotions running high and changing fast. Often a child has real difficulty handling all the thoughts and feelings washing over him and has no idea how to express his overwhelmed state.

That's where you come in.

Nobody Wins All the Time

Though I know there are some educational and social trends that are focused on making every child feel like a winner all of the time, that just doesn't reflect the reality of life. Believe me, I wish we could all feel on top of our games all of the

Nanny Tip

Keep easy-to-play games around the house—checkers, chess, or Go Fish cards. When you win, walk through the process modeling grace: "Thanks for playing. That was fun." And when you lose, model good sportsmanship: "Congratulations. You played a great game."

Cover your dining table with butcher paper one night and put crayons at everyone's place setting before or after serving the meal. Play games like tic-tac-toe with your seat partner, or a family group game like *Pictionary*. Or try to draw pictures of each other without looking down at the page. Creative play not only teaches good sportsmanship but adds the all-important element of fun to your family!

time, especially at heartbreaking moments—like when Fraser was on the ground crying hysterically because he missed a basket. Boy, did I wish I could fly away into a fantasy world of "everybody wins" at that moment. Instead, I had to get down in the dirt, so to speak, and help Fraser deal with the agony of defeat in the most gracious way possible.

When you compete, there is a winner and a loser—and by the time your child completes grade school, he will have had the chance to experience both roles. When (not *if*) your child loses at something, you will want to teach him how to handle it in the early years—so when he's a pro athlete, you won't have to worry about him getting arrested for slugging the ump.

I've always taught my charges that there are three reasons we lose in competitions: sometimes we lose because our skills need improvement, sometimes we lose because we need more play experience, and sometimes it's just a matter of chance. When there is fair play and healthy competition, the third reason is usually the case.

Healthy Competition

Under the basketball scoreboard of my friend's Christian college is the phrase "Audience of One". The school underscores that all players should do their best on the court and off the court, win or lose with grace, and ultimately play to an audience of one—God. Healthy competition takes place in an environment where children are encouraged to play fair and to the best of their abilities; and though, in the end, the final outcome consists of a winner and a loser in terms of the numerical score, they can always walk out of a game a winner to themselves and to God.

One of the most quoted lines in sports movie history is when Eric Liddell, the Olympic runner whose story is portrayed in *Chariots of Fire*, says, "I believe God made me for a purpose, but He also made me fast. And when I run, I feel God's pleasure." The movie is a long one, but I would recommend renting it and playing at least this one scene for your blossoming athlete. Talk with your child about the joy of running well for the sake of moving your body, which is wonderfully made. Talk about the pleasure of making a basket or a hockey goal, or landing a perfect ten on the gymnastic mat, as well as the fun of working with your teammates and watching yourself improve, bit by bit, practice by practice. Yes, we all love to win the game. But the biggest "kick" in life is to enjoy our efforts and to be grateful for the gift of strong legs and arms and mind and talent that allow us to enter into competition.

I don't think I would have been able to stick with it and been proud of who I am and be feminine out on the court. I think I would have folded to the peer pressure if I didn't have my mom to encourage me to be me and be proud of how tall I am.
—Lisa Leslie

You can also help create an attitude of healthy competition for your child in the following ways:

Focus more on effort than outcome through positive, purposeful praise. When your kid kicks the ball but misses the goal, a comment like "What a strong kick!" makes your child's good effort a priority and the outcome secondary.

Focus on strengths. Don't compare siblings or teammates. Each has unique skills and strengths and weaknesses. Focus on the strenghts of the individual. "Wow, you have such grace when you skate!"

Focus on fun. Make playing fun. Take the stress off your child by using humor, playfulness, and a lighter approach to competition. These are, after all, just games. They are not life or death. (Though from the faces of angry and overzealous parents and coaches, one would sometimes think that kids are on the field doing heart surgery on one another.) Come up with a team cheer; invite the kids over for a cookout after the game. Have drills that are fun and all-inclusive. Don't forget to laugh!

Focus on behavior. Stay in tune with your child's pre- and postgame attitude and see if it needs an adjustment. Take note if your child becomes a ball hog or a sore sport, and discuss it. "Why don't you like to pass? For a team to work, everyone needs to do their part." "Can you tell me how you might behave in a more respect-ful way the next time the coach tells you to sit on the bench?"

Focus on teamwork. A team is only as strong as its weakest member. Teach your child that every individual makes a contribution—make yours count! Encourage your child always to do his best. Assure your child that you are watch-ing him with pride whether he is scoring the winning run or cheering on his teammates from the sideline.

Nanny Tip

Don't minimize the character trait of resiliency—it will not only help your children persevere in sports and competitions, but it gives them the ability to overcome obstacles and move forward in a fulfilling life. Teach persistency by working on a challenging puzzle together over several evenings. Build a complicated model or an outdoor tree house, or make a quilt—any activity that takes time, patience, and persistence to complete.

Looking for a Few Good Sports Moms and Dads

Your child will look to you to deter-mine his reactions to life's situations. This is especially important in the com-petitive arena. Kids are too often exposed to inappropriate behavior by disgruntled parents who are frustrated by their child's coaches or referees or even the skills of their own child. Hardly a season goes by that we don't hear of some parent being arrested for unruly conduct at a child's sporting event. Some towns and cities have gone so far as to ban parents from attending championship games in fear of parental outbursts. With all the negative examples out there, it's up to you to model good sportsmanship for your kids.

When I was young, my mom was in a bowling league. She also umpired pro-fessional softball. I was given a wonderful advantage by watching my mother dis-play good sportsmanship right in front of my young eyes. Truly she was in a league of her own! If you or your spouse plays on a city or church league, you have a great chance to model good sportsmanship in front of your children.

I can't tell you how interesting it was the first time my charges accompanied me to my basketball game. They cheered me on as I missed a basket (or two, or three . . .) and even complimented my sportsmanship skills when we lost 30–2. "Wow, Shell, you shake hands good! Nice work." They took note of every hateful look, each argument with the referee, and any inappropriate language that was dis-

> ### *Nanny Tip*
>
> Having a family game night is a perfect opportunity to work on winning and losing as well as teamwork and individual play. It provides an opportunity to be an active role model while giving you tons of natural learning moments.

played, giving me the play-by-play of good versus bad behavior afterward. (They are at the developmental age where playing by the rules is all-important.)

Even if you don't play team sports and you aren't up for trying, you can still show sportsmanlike conduct in lots of little ways. How do you treat the repairman who makes a mistake? Do you behave rationally when watching sports on TV? (By "behave rationally," I don't mean that you don't show normal sports-fan emotion. I just mean you don't use foul language or throw a beverage can across the room and then expect your son or daughter to use self-control on the playing field.)

Here are some other ways you can model good sportsmanship in daily life:

Respect authority. Accept the rulings of the officials without arguing. Officials are only human, and they can and will make mistakes. Next time you're watching a big-league game, observe how you react to what you feel is a blatantly wrong call. Is this how you'd want to see your child react to an official? Or if you get pulled over for speeding, do you argue with the officer, or do you act respectfully? Your kids are sponges, soaking it all up.

Respect your opponents. Treat your opponents the way you want to be treated. Don't taunt your competitors. Don't make fun of their skills or their uniforms. At the end of the game, say, "Thanks for playing," and shake hands. When watching a game with your child, observe positive and negative behaviors toward opponents and point them out and talk about them.

Don't give up—persistence pays off. You won't have a chance to win if you quit. Be an example of a person who doesn't give up easily because of minor setbacks. Treat each defeat as a learning experience. Tell your child that we all fail sometimes. Life isn't about how many times you fail; it's about how many times you get back up. Those who see every rejection, defeat, or setback as a stepping-stone toward improvement and success are the people who realize their dreams.

Every strike brings me closer to the next home run.
—Babe Ruth

Win gracefully. When you win, enjoy it without bragging. Thank the others for taking part in the activity and for playing a good, fair game. Take pride in doing your best and enjoy the victory, but not at the cost of others' feelings.

Lose gracefully. Accept the defeat without pouting. Evaluate the loss and look for things you can improve on for the next time.

Helping Your Kids Find Their Talent

Once you're confident that you are setting an example of good sportsmanship, there are several things you can do to encourage your child to follow in your footsteps.

Be realistic about your child's skill level. Keep your child in appropriate sporting levels. There is no need to put your son in farm league when he is really only ready for T-ball. Why push him beyond his capabilities? It will only cause discouragement and frustration.

Be realistic about your child's level of enthusiasm. Who really enjoys the game: you or your child? Does your child want to play hockey, or do *you* want him to play?

Does he cry before every practice? While it's important to teach a child not to give up, if he is distressed over participating in an activity, you need to find out why. The Bible talks about training a child in the way he is bent,[1] meaning that your job is to observe your child's gifts, interests, and personality traits and encourage his growth in areas where he can experience the most natural joy and success.

Identify your child's strengths and build on them. Everyone has a natural talent. It is important to identify what your child is good at and give him opportunities to use and develop those God-given abilities. For some, it's endurance, which makes them easily excel at running long distances. For others, it's their attention to detail and precision. Games such as chess and sports such as golf build on these qualities and allow them to shine. For the child who has a special love for animals, horseback riding may spark her interest. For the child who has a beautiful voice, taking part in school or church choir may be just her thing. Every child has at least one thing that he does well, and you can help him figure out just what that is.

Some children prefer sports that don't rely heavily on teammates but allow them to compete with themselves or against nature—such as skiing, fishing, rock climbing, kayaking, track-and-field events, golf, dance, or aerobics. Others who are more social thrive in sports involving interaction and competition: volleyball, basketball, baseball, or soccer. As long as your child is engaged in some physical activity that she enjoys, encourage her natural gift—even if it isn't your personal preference.

Support and encourage your children to do their best from beginning to end. Give positive, purposeful praise and encourage perseverance. Give kudos to the kid who plays hard, even when his team is losing. Teach your child that it's about the journey, not just the destination. Instilling the values of follow-through and perseverance in your children will enable them to succeed in the real world—to press on when it might have been much easier to give up.

Remind your child to play hard until the very last second of the game, because "it ain't over till it's over." I just saw my beloved Patriots lose a play-off game to the Broncos, and one particular play during that game will serve as an example to football players everywhere to never slow down until the play or the game is over.

One of the Broncos intercepted the ball and ran for what would have been record-breaking yardage, but he slowed down just before a Patriot defensive player came out of nowhere and tackled him on the one-yard line. If he'd kept running full speed ahead, what a touchdown to remember that would have been! Instead, it was the touchdown that got away.

Encourage good role models. Point out good sportsmanship in the professional arena. Encourage your child to look up to athletes who have a proven track record of being good sports and setting good examples on the field and off.

Do not tolerate inappropriate behavior. If your child drops a swear word or acts inappropriately or disrespectfully, immediately correct the behavior. (Of course, if

 ## *Rules of Good Sportsmanship*

1. Treat others the way you want to be treated.
2. Respect your teammates and your opponents.
3. Respect your coaches and the game officials.
4. Respect the rules of the game, and make sure everyone knows them from the get-go.
5. Always play fair. No cheating—admit if you made a mistake or got called safe when you were really out.
6. Accept the judgment calls of the coaches and the officials without argument.
7. Support and encourage your teammates, even when they make mistakes.
8. Forgive yourself when you make a mistake, and then get right back into the game.
9. Accept defeat with grace. No pouting, no whining, no complaining.
10. Accept victories with grace. No bragging, no making fun of the other team, no gloating.

he's under the supervision of a coach, you'll need to wait until after the game to address it, and hopefully the coach will have already done that.) Impose a consequence for unfair play or the use of rude language.

Take the stress off. Make playing fun. Encourage friendship building in sports and activities.

Coach Creep

Sometime while your child is participating in sports, you'll likely come across a coach who doesn't adhere to the rules of good sportsmanship himself. He may encourage unfair play, exercise favoritism by playing only the best athletes, or even yell and scream when "his kids" fail and miss the mark.

When this is the case, you have to step up to bat for your kid. If you notice that your child is withdrawing from an activity that he usually loves or comes down with a sudden cold five minutes before game time, ask open-ended questions. "How is Coach?" "How's the team?" You may not get a straight verbal answer, but your child's body language will clue you in.

You may even observe for yourself that during a game, some things just don't sit right with you. If you have concerns about the coach, ask yourself these questions:

- Does the coach display patience?
- Does the coach seem to enjoy working with kids?
- Does the coach have reasonable expectations for the age and skill level of his team?
- Does the coach display a positive attitude and emphasize good and fair play as much as winning?

If you answered no to any one of these questions, it's time to speak up. Here's how:

- Observe a practice or a game.
- Make specific mental notes of your concerns. *He whipped the basketball at the wall when the kids didn't do the drill correctly.*
- Call the school guidance counselor or an experienced, trusted sport parent and ask about the coach's previous experience and track record. Have any parents complained? Have there been any previous issues?
- Call the coach's office and ask to set up a meeting.
- Approach the coach with a problem-solving attitude. "I noticed at practice yesterday, the kids couldn't follow the drill instructions and you seemed angry." Tell the coach exactly what he did that you believe was inappropriate. "Can I tell you a bit about my son and what approach might motivate him more effectively?"
- If the coach isn't responsive or acts defensively, use a more direct approach and state your concerns outright. "I feel uncomfortable when you throw the ball at the wall because it displays anger in an environment that is supposed to be fun." "I am not comfortable with the level of emphasis put on winning."
- If you don't see a change, appeal to a higher authority. Even if you do see a change, it's a good idea to talk to the superior about what's going on.

The goal in this is to focus on your child's needs, not play a behind-the-scenes game of "attack the coach." Your child needs to be taught the proper skills and attitude to play the game. If all else fails, it may be time to find another coach or put your child on another team.

 ### Scene 10: Take 2
In the Driveway Playing Basketball

SAM. Come on, you cheated! Mom, Henri is cheating again!
MOM. Henri, was it Sam's turn? Give him the ball back.

HENRI. But I want another shot. I *never* win at this game.

MOM. Henri, you know the rules. When your turn is over, it's over. The game is no fun if you don't play fair.

SAM. Mom! No fair! He's cheating. It's my turn. He wants an extra chance.

MOM. Sam is right, Henri. You aren't following the rules, and if you don't follow the rules, people aren't going to want to play with you. If you don't play, you can't win. Now play by the rules and give your brother the ball, or don't play at all.

HENRI. Fine. Here. I'll wait my turn.

MOM. Thanks, Henri. I don't like it when you don't play fair.

HENRI. Yes, Mom.

MOM. I appreciate your answering me with a respectful tone, even though I know you are disappointed with giving up a turn.

 ### Nanny to the Rescue Again! Recap

What made this mom be a ref of success?

1. *She emphasized the importance of playing by the rules.* Cheating is not OK. It is also not fun. The game is only worth playing if you are playing fair.

2. *She focused on the process, not the outcome.* She didn't focus on Henri's "I never win" comment but rather focused on the process it takes to get there. "If you don't play fair, you don't play. If you don't play, you don't have a chance to win."

3. *She insisted on fair play.* "We play fair, or we don't play at all."

4. *She shared the reality of what can happen if you don't play fair.* No one wants to play with someone who doesn't play by the rules.

5. *She praised a respectful attitude.* When Henri addressed her with respect in spite of his disappointment over her call, she applauded that.

SECTION
THREE

HELP FOR THE HOME FRONT

CHAPTER ELEVEN

CAN'T STOP, WANNA DROP?

 Scene 11: Take 1
Mom on the Phone with Grandma

GRANDMA. Grandpa and I miss you and the kids. Can we see you soon
for dinner?

MOM. Let's see. Monday? Nope. Basketball. Tuesday? No, I forgot Janie
has a playdate. Hmm. Thursday is out. Friday is the big game at
the school, and Saturday everyone is everywhere and I'm still working
out how to get them there.

GRANDMA. Well, what about Sunday?

MOM. No way. That's my only day of rest, and I want to keep it that way.

GRANDMA. Honey, are you OK? You sound worn out. That schedule
seems hectic.

MOM. I've got to go get Cathy off to karate. I'll call you later.

Baseball, basketball, ballet. Spanish, soccer, skating. Boy Scouts, Girl Scouts, my house, your house. So goes a day in the life of many American households, with children juggling schedules fuller than a CEO's day planner.

My mom and I were reminiscing the other day over the way things used to be. "Whatever happened to those days when neighborhood kids played in one another's backyards until the streetlights came on?" she asked. I nodded in agreement.

When did kids stop catching fireflies and start catching taxis?

What occurred in the minds of American parents that took our children from the hopscotch days of yesteryear to the fast track of overachievement? It's like we are collectively frightened there might be a sport our child might not ace (call in the personal trainer!), a band instrument that goes unplayed, or a recital somewhere that our prodigy isn't participating in. And then, oh my goodness, what will happen?

God does not judge us by the multitude of works we perform, but how well we do the work that is ours to do. The happiness of too many days is often destroyed by trying to accomplish too much in one day. We would do well to follow a common rule for our daily lives— DO LESS, AND DO IT BETTER.
—Dale Turner

Our kids will figure out how to make their own fun in their own innovative and creative ways—that's what will happen. And there's an added bonus: you may get to stay home and take a guilt-free nap.

Typically, today's "day" doesn't come to a natural slowing down once the school bell rings. It's only the beginning of a long evening. Practice for this, lessons for that. Free time is no longer free. Parents are shelling out big bucks to make sure that every spot of time is filled with yet one more learning experience—taught by a pro.

I empathize. When all the other kids are on the same trendy treadmill, the pressure is on and the options are wide open and growing every day. It can be disorienting and dizzying. You can find lessons for anything at any time—from a sushi-making class for first graders to seminars titled "How Kids Can Make a Mint on the Internet." (Which, come to think of it, might be a good idea. The family is definitely going to need the cash to pay for all those lessons—or for anti-anxiety medications.)

> ### Nanny Tip
>
> Before signing your child up for a new activity or a new set of lessons, check your motive. Are you doing this for you or for your child? There are few things sadder than watching parents living vicariously through their child.

Where is the time left for a kid to be a kid? Children need time to run and play at their leisure. To search for bugs, fish for tadpoles, lie on their backs, and watch the clouds roll by. They need unhurried time to discover who they are and what their interests are, without the ever-present selective guidance of their parents.

Honestly Evaluate Your Schedule

If you feel like your days are never ending, jam-packed with activities or events, and your Palm Pilot is working on overdrive—put on the brakes of your fast-forward brain for just one moment. It's time to step back and evaluate. To analyze and prioritize. To hit Delete without guilt.

We fear doing too little when we should do more. Then atone by doing too much, when perhaps we should do less.
—Robert Trout

Let's begin by asking some honest questions. Don't worry; no one will see the answers. This is a time for you to be totally honest with yourself—for your sake and for your children's sanity.

Why Am I Doing So Many Things?

Let's face it: many of us are overachieving adults turned into overachieving parents or caregivers. We may need to mentally put ourselves through a "recover your life" program. One of the adages you hear in any sort of twelve-step recovery program is "Check your motives." Here are some questions to help you do just that.

Why are you putting your family through these nonstop hoops? What is your motive for your maddening schedule? Are you giving in to pressure to keep up with the prodigy next door? Did a noble attempt to broaden your child's horizons go haywire somewhere along the way? Do you feel guilty or lazy if you have white spaces on your family calendar, with nothing planned? Are you trying to give your child every advantage because you feel that you were somehow deprived? Do you say yes too often simply because you can afford it (and perhaps your parents could not)?

Another trap is living your dreams through your child, who may or may not share your enthusiasm for a subject, sport, or art. Maybe your child really, truly doesn't want to play the piano, but the pressure from you is too great to decline. Maybe you want your son to play football because all the men in your family know how to pass and tackle. Perhaps your child would prefer to go fishing or build a play fort after school and on weekends. Would your child have the freedom to tell you that he prefers to have his afternoons free to do his own creative projects rather than participate in a competitive sport or take violin lessons? Would he sense your disappointment if he even broached the subject?

> *As the great philosopher Winnie the Pooh said so well, "Don't underestimate the value of Doing Nothing, of just going along, listening to all the things you can't hear and not bothering."*

Are These Activities Making a Positive Impact on My Child?

Is your child's self-esteem getting built up or torn down by participating in an activity? Are the lessons, sports, or extracurricular activities providing positive experiences that seem to refuel your child's inner tank? (Do your children seem happier, more energized, and generally at ease?) Or do you notice some "hurried child" symptoms, such as tears, agitation, exhaustion, and stress?

Do These Activities Take Away from Things That Should Be Higher Priorities?

Is your child's schoolwork suffering because she is doing too much? Is there enough built-in margin (unscheduled time) in your child's life? Does she have time to relax? To read? To be read to? To play with friends? To eat dinner slowly and enjoy sitting at the table conversing with the family?

> ### Nanny Tip
>
> Before signing your child up for long-term lessons, whatever they may be, ask for a trial lesson or two to make sure that your child is really interested in learning the subject, sport, or instrument and that the child and the teacher are a good match.

What Are Our Family's Priorities?

Are family sit-down meals constantly put on the back burner? Do you find yourself asking your child, "What kind of burger do you want at the drive-through?" more often than, "Would you pass the peas, please?" Do you spend more waking hours in your car than in your home?

Does traveling with the team on weekends interfere with the family camping trip that you would normally take? Do the siblings resent having to travel to team games every weekend for the sake of one child's participation? Do you give as much, or more, praise for earning an A on a school project as you do for making a winning goal? Do good grades in school come before good moves on the court?

Analyzing the Answers

So you've made it through the artillery of questions, and perhaps now you have some insight into what's happening and why. Maybe you've seen that the struggle that it takes to get your son ready for a hockey practice (that he doesn't really want to go to) isn't quite worth it simply because you love the sport. Maybe you've come to see that the enrichment you hoped to achieve by providing experiences in the arts, sports, and the other six classes your child is enrolled in has actually drained your family instead.

Only Imagine . . .

The next exercise is to imagine how you'd like to see your family life run, at a pace that gives you plenty of time to enjoy one another and do nothing at all. Imagine waking up to the smell of bacon and eggs, getting everyone off to school smoothly, attending a small and sane smattering of sports or special events for each child, perhaps taking tennis lessons (cooking class, Bible study) together as a family once a month, eating dinner together promptly at six o'clock while sharing about the day's events, relaxing in the evening with homework or a good book, followed by bedside chats and nighttime prayers. Maybe my daydream of a perfect family week is a far cry from yours, but create your own "dream week" in your mind. The details may differ, but most couples want to function as a family team, talking about what's happening, enjoying outings (and evenings at home) together, and running a house like a smooth-sailing ship.

Have a time and place for everything, and do everything in its time and place, and you will not only accomplish more, but have far more leisure than those who are always hurrying.
—Tryon Edwards

Now think about one change you can make in your family's life each week for the next couple of months to bring you closer to that dream. What can you cross off? Are there activities that you can multitask? What could you add to provide greater relaxation or togetherness? Is there anything you can hire out or barter that would free you up to do more of what you want?

Recover Your Family's Life

Here are some tips to help you recover your family's life:

Make a list of all the things you are doing. Evaluate, prioritize, consolidate, and eliminate. By analyzing your daily activities, you'll have a better under-standing of where your time is spent.

Limit your child's extracurricular activities to no more than two per week. Balance athletic activities with creative ones. The more children you have, the more important it is to limit their activities, or you will literally be living in the car and on sports bleachers.

> *Duty makes us do things well, but love makes us do them beautifully.*
> —Zig Ziglar

Let your child choose what specific activities to participate in. Then be sure to encourage him by attending.

Make each Sunday (or Saturday) family day. Attend a church service together, then go out to lunch or have a picnic in the park (or even on your living room floor). Make pancakes on Saturday morning, finish chores early, and then celebrate a job well done by going to the zoo or a concert or in-line skating. Or set up the croquet or badminton set and play in your own backyard.

Have a weekday game night or story night. Find a fun activity that everyone can participate in together and enjoy some good ol' family time. Almost any age of child enjoys listening to one chapter a night (or maybe three nights a week) from a "big book" classic—like *Little House in the Big Woods*, *The Box Car Child*, or *James and the Giant Peach*.

Make eating dinner together a priority. All the experts agree that family meal-time is food not only for the body but also for the mind and soul. I know a fam-ily who looks forward to every Thursday evening as Chinese takeout night. Have one night of the week for each person in the family to help plan the menu (for example, Monday night—Matt's Mealtime Madness, Saturday night—Steven's Supper Surprise).

Have an evening prayer time, even if it's short and sweet. I once worked for a family who sat down before bed each night and allowed each family member to share what they were thankful for. It was cute and insightful to hear the report from the mouths of babes. My agent, Greg Johnson, used to sit on each of his son's beds every night for a short time of father-son talk and prayer. Then after he'd say good night, the boys would listen to the Adventures in Odyssey audio series as they drifted to sleep. In fact, Greg told me that his twenty-year-old son just asked for the whole series as a Christmas present—not only to listen to them again (to relive childhood memories) but to have them for his own children someday. And both boys still call their dad for regular father-son chats. Relational habits, like regular time to listen to your child, will yield a rich, lifelong relationship with your children later on.

Encourage free time. When my charges were in school, every Tuesday was free day. We'd say in the morning, "After school, it's just me and you." They came home and did what they wanted: they played, rested, snuggled, watched a video, built LEGO castles, read, or used the computer. Pbskids.org has some great fun games for younger ones, and we used the computer together. (But they were young. For older kids who prefer to surf the Internet alone, be sure to put a filter on the computer and monitor their time spent and sites visited. Keep the computer in the family room or living room, not in their bedrooms, to be extra cautious.) On our free days, sometimes the boys wanted me in on the action; other times they just wanted to be alone. Often they'd fall asleep knowing they had the freedom and time to catch up on their z's.

Get to know your neighbors. If your neighbors have kids who are around the same age as yours, foster friendship building by having summer barbecues to get to know one another, then make your backyard welcome to your new friends. Encourage your kids to yell over the fence, "Hey, we're outside until dinnertime—come on over!" There's nothing like a spontaneous pickup basketball game with neighborhood kids.

And don't forget the tried-and-true pastimes of hopscotch and catching fireflies in a jar. Think back on your childhood and that of your parents, and have some old-fashioned fun in this fast-forward world.

Scene 11: Take 2
Mom on the Phone with Grandma

GRANDMA. Grandpa and I miss you and the kids. Can we see you soon
for dinner?

MOM. Let's see. Monday? Nope. Basketball. Tuesday? No, I forgot Janie has a
playdate. Hmm. Thursday is out. Friday is the big game at the school,
and Saturday everyone is everywhere and I'm still working out how
to get them there.

GRANDMA. Honey, are you OK? You sound worn out. That schedule
seems hectic.

MOM. Wow, Mom, our schedule does seem pretty crazy now that I hear
myself reciting it.

GRANDMA. Remember when you and your brothers used to just play after
school in the neighborhood—building forts, playing hide-and-seek,
catching ladybugs and grasshoppers till sundown?

MOM. Those were wonderful days! I hate to think my children may be
missing out on being kids. I wonder if I'm raising hurried children,
like the psychologists warn about!

GRANDMA. OK, you know I try to stay out of this kind of thing,
but I really encourage you to take back your life and enjoy some
free evenings and old-fashioned fun. Life's too short not to relax
and enjoy it.

MOM. You're right. I've got to cut back. I'll call you later this evening after the
kids are in bed, and we'll make a date for sure. Maybe you and Dad
can tell me how you did it with us. I had a wonderful childhood and
never felt like I was missing out!

Nanny to the Rescue Again! Recap

What made this mom see that her schedule wasn't all it was cracked up to be?

1. *She saw that her priorities weren't right.* She had no time to spend with those she loved and enjoyed being with.

2. *She had to plan weeks in advance to see her own family.* She didn't like that feeling. Family get-togethers shouldn't have to be scheduled months in advance.

3. *She was overwhelmed trying to do it all.* She can't do it all, and that means her kids can't either. She realized there has to be a better way.

4. *She committed to figuring out why things weren't the way she wanted.* She realized she had to cut back and determined to seek advice and get some help in doing so. If you don't have a mom or grandmother or other mentor, consider setting a few appointments with a life coach, with the goal of adding more flexibility to your family schedule.

CHAPTER TWELVE

ALLOWANCE, CHORES, AND OTHER MONEY MATTERS

 ### *Scene 12: Take 1*
At the Breakfast Nook

ANDY. Mom, if I get an A on my spelling test, can I have five dollars?

MOM. Why do you need five dollars?

ANDY. I want to go to the movies with Kenny this weekend, and that's how Kenny earns his money.

MOM. Yeah, but what happens if Kenny gets a B?

ANDY. He makes sure he doesn't. He really wants the money, so he studies extra hard.

MOM. Oh, I see. So what happens if his mom doesn't agree to give him the money?

ANDY. I'm not sure, but I guess he wouldn't study as hard.

From an early age, children like to feel they are a part of helping the family home run smoothly. You may remember the time your preschooler surprised you by proudly announcing, "I cleared the dishes from the table all by myself!" while you were in the bathroom, only to discover that this meant he threw all of the food, along with the plates and silverware, in the trash! You didn't know whether to laugh or to cry, but you applauded his efforts because you knew he was trying, and the last thing you wanted to do was squelch his first feeble efforts.

Kids want to feel they have a place to belong, and they enjoy having and fulfilling assigned responsibilities. They want to contribute and feel, "What I do is important too!" Capitalizing on these natural impulses is one of the big secrets to getting your kids to be good helpers around the house from age two to age twenty. *Life Skills for Kids* by Christine Field is a great book on teaching children in simple steps with increasing levels of responsibility about what they'll need to know to survive in the real world.[1]

If you want children to keep their feet on the ground, put some responsibility on their shoulders.
—Abigail Van Buren

Parents have different opinions on assigning chores. Some feel kids should have them; others don't. Some feel that children should receive payment for doing these assigned tasks; others don't. Although the argument about financial payment for chores is debatable, what isn't debatable is that children feel valued when their contributions to the family team are acknowledged by a pat on the back or verbal praise. "Wow, you did a fabulous job on this backyard cleanup!"

Chores for Cash?

My personal opinion about whether to pay your child for doing chores has always been that these maintenance activities are part of life, part of learning to take responsibility for yourself and your environment. Because of this, I don't think children should be financially compensated for the basic chores that contribute to the family team.

I feel that the best compensation comes from a job well done. So while I don't think it's a valuable lesson to compensate children financially for what they should be doing anyway, I do believe they should be encouraged in other ways, particularly with verbal praise. "Great job!" "I so appreciate your help!"

Create a Chore Chart

A great (and easy) idea to keep track of the pack is using a chore chart. A whiteboard is ideal because it can be changed and updated easily and takes very little maintenance. You can make a chart with each child's name and task, and your kids can check off their chores as they are accomplished.

You can also use a magnetic list on your fridge. Create a chore list on a large piece of paper and place it on the fridge. Get a set of magnets for each child (the ones with names really work great), and put the magnet next to the tasks that

It is important to make sure you are assigning age-appropriate chores that your children have the mental and physical abilities to complete. Here is a list of helpful tasks that children ages six through twelve can do with appropriate guidance and supervision.

- Make their beds
- Carry laundry to and from the laundry area
- Put their own laundry away
- Help care for animals
- Do general tidying up
- Set the table
- Clear the table
- Load and unload the dishwasher
- Help carry and put away groceries
- Help cook simple foods
- Help wash and vacuum the car
- Vacuum, sweep, and mop
- Clean the bathroom
- Rake leaves
- Take out the trash

they are responsible for. Have them take their magnet off and put it to the side when the task has been completed.

You can even print out free, designed chore charts at www.chartjungle.com and use the tried-and-true gold star system.

Money Matters

Helping children learn the value and management of money is a priceless life lesson. From an early age, children observe how you handle your money and are curious to know what you spend it on. Whether you realize it or not, you are their first and most important role model for money management.

As I shared before, I'm not keen on the idea of paying children for things like good grades, basic household chores, or other family tasks that are just part of life's routine. However, kids do need some ways to earn money so that you can help them learn how to manage it. Most kids are eager to earn money by doing additional work, outside the routine chores. In fact, you might post a list of these odd jobs and what you are willing to pay your child to do them. Call it the "extra jobs chart," and list things

The Four "S" Budget System

One good and easy budgeting system is to divide your child's allowance money into the four "S" categories: *spend now*, *spend later*, *save*, and *send*.

The *spend now* money is for the here and now, for things like school lunch, snacks, and other daily needs. The *spend later* money is designated for the purchase of an item that your child wants. The *save* money is the money to be set aside in case of emergencies or for later in life. The *send* money is set apart for charity, church, or other giving.

like helping to organize the closets, supervising younger siblings while you are getting housework or phone calls done, mowing the lawn, or other "above and beyond" tasks. Come up with a mutually agreed-on fee, and put that kid to work! Then when they ask, "Hey, Dad, can I have five dollars to go to the movie?" you can say, "Go check the extra jobs chart and see what you can do to earn it!"

Allowance for Allowances

Though I don't like to tie allowances in with normal daily chores, I see high value in teaching kids the importance of creating and managing a budget.

I owe this idea to a mom friend who shared it with me as we were visiting in the park one day, the kids playing around us. I really liked it and adapted her method to fit our family. For each of her children, she gave the equivalent in dollars to their grade in school. For example, their third-grade child got three dollars per week, and their fifth-grade child got five dollars per week.

She then went on to share her money-management model. Their allowance was to be divided in the following way:

Nanny Tip

Once your child shows a true interest in money, take him to a local kid-friendly bank and open a savings account. He can deposit his birthday check from Grandma, his earnings, or part of his allowance and learn to keep track of and budget his funds. He can learn about interest and learn how money is a cycle of exchanging services for cash and cash for things; but most of all, he will learn that money doesn't grow on trees.

- 10 percent church offering
- 10 percent college
- 10 percent savings (must be saved for six months before using)
- 20 percent taxes (she felt they might as well get used to it)
- 50 percent discretionary

Their college and tax money got deposited into a savings account in their name to be used for college later. The discretionary money could be spent however they wished, and their savings was put into a piggy bank. I had to agree that this model instills good habits and budgeting skills in even the earliest earners.

When kids have money of their own to spend, they will quickly and quite naturally develop a sense of prioritizing. They will learn the difference between their wants and their needs. Of course, they will flub up a few times and think a want is actually a need. But don't we all still do that?

Free to Spend . . . and Sometimes Fail!

When it comes to discretionary spending, it's often best to keep criticism to yourself. Praising your children's positive efforts instead of critiquing their mistakes is almost always a more productive practice. After all, making mistakes is part of any learning process.

Let's say your son buys a box of fruit yogurt popsicles with his own money so he can enjoy a special cold treat on hot summer days. Then, say, he eats the whole box in an hour. The tummy ache and the lack of treats to look forward to the rest of the week will be a valuable lesson. My personal opinion is that unless you think natural consequences will do real damage, allow them to serve their purpose.

Also, you may think it wise that your child spend her own three dollars (from a gift or earnings) on a practical, pretty set of stationery. But if your daughter wants to spend it on a gaudy necklace that she absolutely adores (in disastrous shades of purple, green, and black), you need to allow her to express her own taste and enjoy these small purchasing freedoms without interference. (And when she wears it on a family outing—beaming with pride at her purchase—you'll just have to suck it up and smile, Mom. Part of letting go is letting your child express her own fashion style—as long as it is within the limits of modesty.)

Finances Are a Family Affair

Including your child in your family's financial planning is also a good way for kids to learn about budgeting realities. Have a monthly meeting where all family members can share how their money management is going, what they are learning, what they have purchased, and what they are saving for. Here are some great topics to talk about in your informal family "money matters" meeting.

It costs money to run a household. Give a general overview of the bills you had to pay that month and how much of the total income basic bills use up. Ask if your children have any ideas about how to possibly reduce some of the bills. Emphasize how many hours you had to work to pay the electric bill or the house payment. Show a one-to-one correspondence between labor and meeting the family's basic needs.

There is a difference between wants and needs. Share some personal stories about this. Hindsight being twenty-twenty, you may be able to help steer your kids away from the same mistakes. Tell them about that faulty get-rich-quick scheme you invested in, under the pressure of a salesperson. Or about the time you made an impulse purchase and ending up paying on it long after the purchase was lost, worn, or forgotten. Hearing about your experiences helps your children see that adults struggle with needs versus wants too. They aren't alone!

All that's plastic isn't free. Share some situations where you charged an item and paid it off over time, and how that process works. (And be sure to teach your kids how the interest rate sneaks up on you!)

Plan fun family outings. During your family meeting, vote on a place to go and make a financial plan for how to get there. Everyone will need to contribute!

Use some books or games for children that will teach them about finances in fun ways. One of the best Web sites for teaching your children about successful investing is www.richkidsmartkid.com. (They offer online games and also a book by the same name, as well as games you can purchase.) Another great Web site with money-management articles and ideas is www.kidsmoney.org.

The old standbys *Monopoly* and *The Game of Life* teach some valuable lessons on business and what it costs to live and raise a family—but these games are so fun that the learning will go down without them noticing. Take advantage of some newer technology, too, such as selling items on eBay (perhaps bought at a garage sale at a bargain price) and allowing your miniature businessman to get a taste of making a profit.

 ### Scene 12: Take 2
At the Breakfast Nook

ANDY. Mom, if I get an A on my spelling test, can I have five dollars?

MOM. Why do you need five dollars?

ANDY. I want to go to the movies with Kenny this weekend, and that's how Kenny earns his money.

MOM. Yeah, but what happens if Kenny gets a B?

ANDY. He makes sure he doesn't. He really wants the money, so he studies extra hard.

MOM. Oh, I see. So what happens if his mom doesn't agree to give him the money?

ANDY. I'm not sure, but I guess he wouldn't study as hard.

MOM. So is that how you feel? You will only do your best if you get paid for it? Isn't feeling good about doing your best good enough?

ANDY. Yeah, but I want to make my own money.

MOM. OK, let me talk to Dad, and we'll figure out how we can work out a win-win deal here. I don't want you to get used to being paid for good grades or doing the basic chores we all have to do in order to work as a team. But it is about time you learned how to manage money of your own, so we'll come up with some fair ideas for how you can earn some dough. Deal?

ANDY. OK! Thanks.

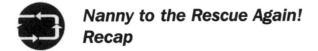

Nanny to the Rescue Again!
Recap

How did this mom deal with her money-hungry son?

1. *She reiterated her family values.* "We don't do our best because we get paid for it. We do our best because it's the right thing to do and it simply feels good to do so!"
2. *She didn't give in to the "But so-and-so does it" protest.* She looked at the situation based on their family values, instead of just going along with what a friend does.
3. *She valued the importance of learning money management.* She decided to talk with her husband and come up with a way for their child to learn how to manage his own funds.

CHAPTER THIRTEEN

WHAT'S HAPPENING TO MY BODY?

 Scene 13: Take 1
After Baseball Practice

(Justin comes in the front door, dragging his feet, despondent over his poor performance at baseball practice.)

MOM. Justin, I know you must really feel sad. Let's sit down and talk about what's going on. I'll make us each a cup of hot cocoa.

JUSTIN, *grumbling.* I just wannagotomyroom.

MOM. Now, Justin, that isn't very nice, is it? I think you really need to sit down with me and talk it out right now. Trust me, you'll feel better.

JUSTIN. Leave me alone! I said I don't want to talk! *(He goes to his room and slams the door.)*

MOM, *in tears, on the phone with Justin's dad.* I don't know what's gotten into that boy! He's so rude to me lately. I have no clue how to reach him since he's hit puberty. It's like an alien lives in our home!

"Though it may appear that hormones have caused your son to go haywire, an adolescent boy's body is not broken. It does not need to be fixed," writes Annette Smith in her book *Help! My Little Boy's Growing Up.*[1] The mood swings, the pull for sudden (and total) independence, a pubescent kid's escalating insistence on privacy—all of this is a normal part of God's design. Although boys usually hit puberty slightly later than girls, it is easy to tell when they are entering the age and stage when their hormones take over their heads.

Your daughter may show signs of entering the "adolescent zone" when she begins reporting on her day at school with soap-opera-like theatrics rather than chatting it up about the A she got on the spelling test. "Jordan wanted to hang out with Sean, but, like, he blew her off and she was *so* bummed that she started flirting with Nate just to get Sean back. But then Nate thought, like, wow, Jordan really likes me! And now . . . ohmygosh, it's a big mess. Jordan and Michelle are coming over after school to talk about what to do next, OK? Would you mind making some brownies? We are definitely going to need *chocolate*!" And off she goes, with a feminine flounce, hands flying as she chats, preparing to dive in to the latest emotional/relational crisis at hand. When did your darling turn into a diva?

Change always comes bearing gifts.
—Price Pritchett

Your preadolescent son, on the other hand, may have suddenly turned monosyllabic. And even those rare syllables can be a challenge to interpret.

"How was your day, honey?"

"Arumphff."

"Sorry, I didn't quite catch that."

But alas, it is too late; he's headed for his "cave," where he'll disappear even more into the music coming from his headphones or a handheld video game. You miss him, but don't worry. He'll be back—just when it's least convenient. He'll be ready to talk to you when he's ready to talk, and that is usually when you are engrossed in a book, trying to juggle ten tasks at once, or otherwise deeply engaged. You may have practically begged your growing son to have a discussion when you were free of distractions, willing and able to give him focused attention, but he didn't respond. However, when you are focusing on something else or heading out the door, late for a meeting, *this* is the time he'll suddenly turn into Mr. Talkative and want your undivided attention.

Welcome to the crazy, hazy, wavy days of puberty.

Because boys and girls have radically different experiences with puberty (it is, after all, the stage that separates the guys from the gals in mighty profound ways), I've decided to divide this chapter into "his" and "her" sections to address the specific coming-of-age issues for each gender.

Her Turn

As friend, humorist, and author Becky Freeman Johnson told me, "Frankly, it's not that easy to be totally upbeat with your daughter about the 'womanly art of menstruation' and still keep a straight face." I had to agree. Not many women I know want to chat endlessly about their periods, as miraculous as the reproductive cycle may be. In fact, Becky describes her first conversation with her daughter, Rachel, as simply leveling with her: "Look, there's something coming on the horizon called a period, and yes, you do have to have one. Every month. Until you are Granny's age or have your uterus removed, whichever comes first." When it comes to the blessings and burdens of becoming a woman, frankness and a good sense of humor will be great allies.

> *Be truthful about menstruation. Periods aren't particularly pleasant, but neither are they awful. They are, in fact, an outside sign that everything inside is working as it should.*
> —Annette Smith

The sooner you talk with your daughter about periods and how babies are made, the better. Girls are starting to menstruate younger and younger, and of course, no matter how protective you are, kids today hear about sex much sooner, and in more detail, than any other generation. Better for her to hear the truth from you than from the girls on the playground where information is iffy and morals may be questionable.

Common Questions About Menstruation

Here are some common questions girls have about menstruation, along with some straight-up answers.

When will I start? Most girls begin having a period between the ages of ten and sixteen, typically between eleven and thirteen years old.

How often does it happen? Near the end of the teen years, a girl's cycles will come about every twenty-eight days. But until then, most girls have very irregular periods.

Does it hurt? Most girls only experience a slight cramping and small amount of discomfort in their abdomen or lower back.

How much blood will I lose? The amount of blood lost each month can range from one to eight tablespoons. The blood is released very slowly over two to eight days and may range in color from light brown to bright red to very dark maroon.

How will it happen, and what will I do? Usually, you will see blood on your underwear, in the toilet, or on the toilet paper. If you start your period and don't have a pad with you, you can ask for one from the nurse or teacher if you are at school. If you are at a friend's house, you can always ask for one from her, her mom, or her older sister.[2]

Adjusting to the Big "P"

On the day (or during the week) your daughter begins her first period, you don't want to embarrass her in any way, but you do want to communicate that you recognize she is now on her way to womanhood, and you want to celebrate and applaud this new era. Perhaps you might give her permission to get her ears pierced or buy her first pair of semi-high-heeled shoes or get a manicure. Then take her to a chick flick and nice girly restaurant, just the two of you.

Make up a "secret language" for dealing with things like tampons and pads and periods. One family of females I know refers to feminine supplies as "rosebuds." Maybe you could call them "pink cotton balls," and then, if your daughter needs you to purchase pads or tampons, and family or friends are around, she can say, "Hey, Mom! Can you get me some of those pink cotton balls I like?" No one is

Cures for Cramps

Some girls have more painful cramps than others, and each is calmed in different ways. Here are a variety of ideas to help your daughter deal with the aches and pains of being a girl.

1. Gently rub your abdomen with lotion warmed in the microwave.
2. Take ibuprofen.
3. Take a multivitamin with iron (be sure she doesn't take this on an empty stomach, however). Be sure to check with her doctor first.
4. Do some slow, warm-up type exercises—with gentle stretches and bending.
5. Try lying on a heating pad or hot water bottle or taking a long, hot soak in the tub. Air-Activated Therapeutic HeatPacks by Cura-Heat are great disposable heating pads that can even be worn discreetly under clothes.
6. Cut back on caffeine or sugar and see if that helps.
7. If your daughter is experiencing terrible pain regularly, take her to a doctor who will have a variety of ways to help. Most girls at this age greatly prefer a female doctor, so if you can find a good female physician, this will probably ease your daughter's growing anxiety about modesty when being examined.

the wiser, it spares her embarrassment, and the two of you are in on a little mom-daughter secret.

Your daughter may get weepy or irritable for no reason in the days before her period. In some homes, PMS stands for Pre-Monster Syndrome. Share ways she can soothe her emotions while assuring her that this blue mood will pass when her hormone levels normalize in a few days. Ask her, "What might make you feel better? A nap? A hot bubble bath? A warm cup of decaffeinated tea?" Teach her to make a little list of things she can do to nurture herself when she's feeling down. Self-soothing is a great skill.

Buying a First Bra

There will come a day when you or your little girl will begin to notice that she's growing "bumps" on her chest (or nature's way of making mountains out of molehills).

When do you take your daughter shopping for a bra? When she asks for one—no matter how small or unobvious the need. Or you may be the one to suggest a shopping trip to the lingerie department when you see she is blossoming and needs some sort of beginner's bra for the sake of modesty. Most girls like shopping for sports bras first; they are comfy and fit almost like mini tank tops. Let her choose something she thinks is fashionable or pretty or cool, using her own sense of style. As we women know all too well, breasts come in all shapes and sizes, so assure your daughter that whatever she grows on her chest will be absolutely perfect!

> **Nanny Tip**
>
> Myfirstbra.com is a great Web site for learning what you need, when you need it, and where to get it!

Between hormones, periods, and shopping for bras, some girls get a bit overwhelmed with the idea of saying good-bye to childhood and growing up so suddenly. To help your daughter through this awkward transition, when she feels part little girl (looking back to her stuffed animal collection with sentimentality) and part preteen (looking forward to dates and driving), allow her to slip into and out of each role as she needs to do so. Don't give up Happy Meals or playing in the park or browsing Toys "R" Us aisles just because she started her period last month. Mingle shopping together for a first pair of earrings with stopping to ooh and aah, in childlike glee, over a cute pile of stuffed animal babies or adorable dolls. Let her be half little girl and half growing young woman—and enjoy them both.

Body Talk

Though space doesn't permit me to go into great detail here, it is imperative that every parent brush up on the basic facts of eating disorders—how they begin, how they can be prevented, and what to look for if you think your child may have one.

> *The best time to help your daughter develop a positive body image is well before the teen years.*
> —Kathleen McCoy, PhD

Every year, the age for girls being hospitalized for severe eating disorders is getting younger and younger. Check out www.empoweredkidz.com—a helpful Web site for young girls and their parents that emphasizes healthy eating habits that may help you prevent an eating disorder from ever taking hold of your child.

A companion Web site is www.empoweredparents.com, originated by author Abigail H. Natenshon, a psychotherapist who has treated children, adults, couples, families, and groups dealing with eating disorders for the past thirty-five years. Her book *When Your Child Has an Eating Disorder: A Step-by-Step Workbook for Parents and Other Caregivers* may be of real help if you have any concerns about significant changes in your child's eating or exercising habits.[3]

Faith-Based Resources for "The Talk"

Girls ages eight through twelve love the popular Lilly series by Nancy Rue. To encourage a young woman to value her body (and insist that boys do the same), try reading *The Body Book—It's a God Thing!* in the Lilly series.[4] Many moms and daughters have enjoyed reading this book together as a way to comfortably intro-duce the subjects of puberty and a spiritually positive view of sex.

Also, check out the God's Design for Sex series by NavPress. Each book is age appropriate, with a helpful parent guide.

- *The Story of Me* is for ages three to five.
- *Before I Was Born* is for ages five to eight.
- *What's the Big Deal* is for boys and girls ages eight to eleven.
- *Facing the Facts* is for kids ages eleven to fourteen.

His Turn

Annette Smith—registered nurse, mother, and author—candidly sums up the situation of boys entering puberty with wit and candor: "Most moms can get away with addressing basic gender-neutral topics like voice changes, body odor and acne, but nearly all boys most emphatically do not care to discuss with their mother any of those matters taking place further south than their armpits."[5]

Calling all dads to read this section! (And if you are a single mom, "Calling all uncles, grandfathers, or big brothers!") Men, your boys need your friendship, empathy, and transparency now more than ever. And your wife needs you to be 100 percent there during this time when your boy is turning into a man, leaning less on his mother and looking more and more to you as his role model.

Here's a potpourri of facts concerning your soon-to-be adolescent son. (Men, if you don't know what potpourri is, ask your wife. I just want to make sure the moms continue to feel needed in this chapter.)

- Sometime between the ages of ten and fourteen, the pituitary gland sets in motion events that boost testosterone, triggering all sorts of changes. It will be between ages sixteen and eighteen that this process is complete.

- Life is hardest on the boys who are late bloomers. Another man who was a late bloomer can encourage your son if he is a little behind the other boys in growth.

- The average adolescent boy nearly doubles his weight between the ages of twelve and sixteen. His height may increase four or more inches in a year (and your grocery bill will increase accordingly!).

- Sweat glands become active during puberty, and you may need to be a little firmer about the need for showers. Purchase him some manly deodorant and cologne to encourage him to stay fragrant. Also keep baking soda handy for him to sprinkle in his shoes. (What mother hasn't practically fainted dead away from the smell of an adolescent boy's socks on laundry day?)

- Though you probably don't want to think about it, this is the age when hair appears—everywhere—and if that's not enough to make you nervous, by this point he will probably experience nocturnal emissions or "wet dreams." Smith says it is a good idea to teach your son to do his own laundry occasionally before puberty, so if the need arises, he can launder his own sheets or underwear without calling unwanted attention to what, for him, will be an embarrassing situation. Respecting his privacy and knocking before entering are going to be increasingly important.[6]

The open access to porn through the easy availability of the Internet and cable TV in homes is like opening a candy store for a diabetic. Use parental controls. Keep the computer in the family room, where anyone can walk by at any time. Check the "history" on your computer's Web browser now and then. If the rules are being violated, better to restrict or even get rid of Internet access and cable channels than put your son within reach of too much temptation.

The amount of testosterone pulsing through an adolescent boy stimulates a battle in his mind and body that probably won't subside until he is . . . oh, about seventy or so. An understanding mom and dad recognize the realities, never shaming their son but encouraging him toward the goal: a beautiful sexual relationship within a committed marriage to the girl of his dreams.

Guy Talk, Interpreted

Dr. William Pollock, researcher and author of *Real Boys*, has some fascinating things to say about how boys communicate. If you are a mom, you'll probably find it a great relief to recognize what's going on inside your son's noggin. "The most challenging time for communication, the time when mothers and sons are most likely to disconnect (although in their hearts they may long to connect even more closely), is when a boy is hurting. I have found that when boys suffer a blow to their self-esteem or otherwise feel sad or disappointed, they often follow a pattern that I call the 'timed-silence syndrome.' "[7]

Pollock explains that a boy's first reaction to pain is to retreat and be alone with his hurt. Of course, every mom's normal response is to want to tend and mend, right? Here's the issue: "If a mother presses him with concerned questions at that point, it only intensifies his sense of shame and causes him to retreat further or more angrily. In many cases, it's only after he has had time to sit with his own pain that he becomes ready to come back and talk about it."[8]

And, moms, when he does come around, it is easy to miss his clues. "At that point his approach may be so subtle that his mother could easily miss it."[9] And if you miss the moment, it may be awhile before he tries to connect with you again.

If your son, for example, had a bad day at school or got rebuffed by a girl, heads straight to his room, and says, "I just want to be left alone"—it is probably best for you to believe him and honor his wishes. He's in his cave licking his wounds. When he is feeling ready to talk, he may quietly appear in the room, without saying much, or just make some small talk. This is your opening that it is now OK to ask him, "So can you tell me a bit about what happened?"

Extra Resources for Dads!

Dad's Everything Book for Sons and *Dad's Everything Book for Daughters* by Greg Johnson and John Trent (Zondervan, 2003) are two very readable, practical books for any father who would like to brush up on his relationship with his eight- to twelve-year-old child.

Man in the Making by Greg Johnson (Broadman and Holman, 1997) is a book that your son can read alone or with you. One reviewer said, "This book has 35 short chapters that get right to the point with concrete, easy-to-relate-to examples. . . . It doesn't talk down to the reader and is a great resource for parents or anyone who works with young men."

She Calls Me Daddy by Robert Wolgemuth (Focus on the Family, 1999) focuses on seven things every father needs to know about raising a complete daughter.

Raising a Modern-Day Knight by Robert Lewis (Focus on the Family, 1999) is an excellent resource for fathers who'd like to help their sons catch a King Arthur–like vision of manhood and godliness.

Every Young Man's Battle by Steve Arterburn and Fred Stoeker (WaterBrook, 2000) is a great book to help fathers prepare their sons for the lifetime battle of reining in their desires with practical tips on how to honor God's gift of sex.

Healthy Guy-Girl Friendships

Once your preadolescent kids have exited the age of cooties, it is amazing how quickly the opposite sex gets *very* interesting to them. Here are a few tips you can share with your child to encourage him or her to form healthy friendships with the opposite sex.

Be yourself. Don't pretend to be someone you aren't to attract a boy or girl. It's too much work, and you can't keep it up forever. Forget about playing dumb— that's a dumb thing to do!

Learn the art of ping-pong conversation. A good conversation goes back and forth fairly equally—some chatting, some attentive listening. Get a book of conversation starters for your preteen boy or girl with questions that require more than a yes or no answer.

Let your presence say "There you are!" instead of "Here I am!" Be happy to see others and try to focus on them before starting in with a long story about yourself.

> ### Nanny Tip ♥
>
> Good, bad, or ugly, your model of marriage is what it is. It's the standard your child will learn to gauge a marriage by. Having a loving, respectful marriage is the most valuable gift you can give your child—it's setting a high standard for your child to strive toward as he enters into adulthood, looking for a mate of his own.

Dress nicely, but avoid "cheap and easy" looks. Yes, guys may stare at a girl wearing a low-cut shirt, but they'll also stare at a train wreck. Girls, strive to look classy but never trashy. If in doubt, don't.

Be a bit mysterious. Girls or guys may tend to put their hearts on their sleeves way too soon—and end up scaring the opposite sex away. There's an art to showing interest in a nice boy or girl yet leaving the other person wondering a bit, wanting to be with you again. Don't tell a guy or girl everything about you all at once. Allow a friendship to unfold slowly and naturally.

Be interesting! The only bored people in the world are *boring* ones. Guys and girls are drawn to people who like life and live it fully. Get interested in astronomy, reading, rock climbing, cooking, music, or whatever sparks your interest, and take classes if you can. You'll find other interesting, self-motivated kids.

Use humor! Everyone loves people who see the funny side of life, so laugh often, but never at another person's expense.

Don't neglect your friends. Sometimes when a boy and girl like each other, they start to pair off and leave their friends behind. Your friends will resent it, and besides, your new friend of the opposite sex needs to know he or she isn't the center of your universe.

Set high standards. Though it may seem too early, a fourth, fifth, or sixth grader is not too young to decide what their physical limitations will be with another boy or girl. It's all about cherishing themselves and their future spouse by setting limits on physical touching or kissing ahead of time (instead of in the heat of the moment). This would be a great subject to ask a youth minister or respected older Christian guy or girl to chat with your child about, just to reinforce your values at home.

Dealing with Dating

The topic of dating is coming up for kids at younger and younger ages. Even young elementary-school children may be starting to pair off into couples. Someday you may experience a conversation with your child that goes something like this:

COLLEEN, *walking into the house after school, sobbing.* He *hates* me!

MOM, *confused.* What's the matter? Who hates you?

COLLEEN. Brandon. He doesn't want to be my boyfriend anymore.

    He likes Karen now.

MOM. Boyfriend? When did you get a boyfriend?

Space doesn't permit me to cover the subject of dating in detail here, but I want you to be prepared to deal with the subject when it comes up with your child—most likely, much sooner than you expect! So here are some tips on dealing with dating:

• Discuss your family philosophy of dating with your spouse.
• Be clear in setting your guidelines and communicating them to your children.
• Encourage your child to have healthy friendships with those of the opposite sex.
• Promote that children hang out in groups, rather than one-on-one.
• Provide a clear understanding of the boundaries under which these
   friendships can blossom.

Though the preteen years can be frightening (for both you and your child), as you can see, there are some fabulous, factual, and faith-based resources to help you through the rapids. Take a little time to do your research, read some of the recommended books, pray for wisdom, and then dive in and enjoy the ride!

 **Scene 13: Take 2
After Baseball Practice**

*(Justin comes in the front door, dragging his feet, despondent over his poor
   performance at baseball practice.)*
MOM. Justin, I'm so sorry you had a bad day.
JUSTIN, *grumbling.* I just wannagotomyroom.
MOM. Sure. Take some alone time. I'll be here in the kitchen if you decide
   you want to talk.
*(Justin, several minutes later, slowly opens his bedroom door, sits down at the
   kitchen counter, and looks out the window blankly.)*

MOM, *looking up and smiling softly.* Hey there, buddy. *(She continues chopping carrots but moves the cutting board closer to him to lessen the distance between them.)* So. How was practice?

JUSTIN. Not good.

MOM. Well, here—peel a carrot and tell me all about it . . .

(They work side by side, listening and talking, comforting, and bonding at a relaxed, unpressured pace.)

 ## Nanny to the Rescue Again! Recap

What did this mom do right with her growing guy?

1. *She respected his need for privacy.* She empathized with her son, but when she saw that he wasn't up to talking further, she respected his need for privacy and regrouping alone.

2. *She let him deal with his emotions at his own pace.* She held back her natural urge to pry, tend, and mend and went about her work, calmly letting her son know that if and when he wanted to talk, she'd be there.

3. *She didn't miss his subtle cues.* She acknowledged him (without dramatic emotion) and moved toward him discreetly, asking a test question before diving in to talk. When he answered, she knew by his face and body language that he was now ready to talk.

4. *She talked while she worked and engaged his help.* This approach met three guy needs: (1) boys usually enjoy talking more if they are also doing something; (2) boys love to feel needed and helpful, which may help heal a bruised manly ego; and (3) the act of peeling carrots together is quiet, repetitive, and relatively mindless, allowing thoughts and conversation to flow.

CHAPTER FOURTEEN

VIRTUES TO GROW ON

 Scene 14: Take 1
At the School Lunch Table

DARLENE. I am so hungry. I forgot to eat breakfast and didn't bring my lunch.

KENDALL. Well, go buy something.

DARLENE. Yeah, of all days, I forgot my backpack on the bus.

KENDALL, *enjoying her homemade lunch.* What a bummer, huh? You're always forgetting something.

DARLENE. I called my mom to ask her to bring me something, but she's not at her desk at work.

KENDALL. Wow, I wish I had some more money, but I only have enough for an ice cream sandwich after I finish what my mom packed.

One of the highest privileges of parenting is passing on your family values to your children by being a solid role model to them. One of my friends, an excellent father, puts it this way: "I want to live in such a way that my child, even as an adult, will continue to come to me when he is struggling or needs advice and allow me the honor of speaking into his life." A high goal, but we all know that no parent can be a perfect role model.

One of the things that helps me balance the desire to be a good role model with my obvious imperfections is that I know I'm not asking others to look to me (or any human being) as their guru on a pedestal. Now, I'm aware I may sometimes sound a bit nanny-guru-ish at times, but I'm very aware that even I can't do all I've suggested you do in this book all of the time. I get tired, have headaches, and endure blue moods too—days when I have to tell my charges, "I'm sorry, but I'm having a hard time getting it together myself today. Be patient with me if you can. God's not finished with me yet!"

The only one we can trust to be loving, kind, patient, and faithful all the time is God. As a Christian, I am on a journey—along with other Christ followers—to try to live my life, as best I can, as I understand Jesus to have lived and loved. Even if your family practices another faith, the virtues of Jesus are pretty universally admired, so I think you'll find these attributes applicable to your family too.

Although there are dozens of Christian virtues to choose from, here is my favorite "nanny eight" to get you started.

Grace

Grace is undeserved favor. It's giving love when it's not necessarily deserved. This is the loving, penetrating look we saw on the face of the actor who played Jesus in *The Passion of the Christ*, which touched viewing audiences so deeply. You may remember a similar look of grace coming from your mother, grandmother, father, or spouse. I hope someone in your life has given you the gift of unconditional acceptance.

God has a divine ability to look beyond bad behavior to the deeper need of every human heart. What a model for us as parents on days when we wonder if we gave birth to the bad seed or wonder if our kids came with any sort of return policy. With God's help, we can pray to look beyond our children's tantrums, backtalk, or teenage rebellion and ask Him to help us see and meet the real, underlying need in our child's heart. As we demonstrate this sort of grace with our kids, they will take note of our tenderness of heart as well.

Encourage your child to show grace by accepting people for who they are. When the teenage babysitter gets her nose pierced, and your kids know you aren't personally wild about piercings, make it clear that her new adornments do not affect how you treat her one bit. You love and respect her and are grateful she doesn't judge you for wearing high-waisted, outdated "mom jeans" either.

Rather than speaking in judgment of homeless people or those who've made public mistakes and are paying for them in painful ways, you can speak with grace. "Sugar, I don't know why that man is begging for money on the corner; only God knows. Perhaps if I had a bad home life or battled alcoholism or wasn't able to get a job or had a mental illness, I might be doing the same thing. There's no way to know. All we can do is pray for every homeless person we see and contribute some time and money to causes that we trust will try to help them get better lives."

Or perhaps there's a rumor going around about a teacher who is going through a divorce—and a variety of rumors as to the reasons. You might say to your child, "Whatever happened in your teacher's marriage to bring her to the point of divorce must have been terribly painful for her whole family. I hope that she has lots of kind and loving and nonjudgmental friends to show their care and compassion in this hard time. I hope you won't do anything to add to your teacher's pain by talking about her in bad ways, OK?"

Give others the benefit of the doubt when you just aren't sure. When fighting over the ball on a jump shot, if you aren't quite sure who got it, give it to the other person.

Forgiveness

Forgiveness is excusing someone from an offense. It's wiping the slate clean from a past hurt and allowing fresh starts. Someone once said, "Forgiveness is like setting a prisoner free and then discovering you were the prisoner after all."

In his book *Forgive for Good*, author Frederic Luskin talks about the uselessness of "renting space in our heads" to nurse old grudges.[1] Who's hurting whom in this case? Usually we are hurting ourselves by replaying old tapes over and over until we have a story of "Somebody done me wrong" that we can recite, word perfect, at will. Luskin calls these "grievance stories," and we all know (and try to avoid) people who have become one big, walking grievance story. They are victims, and they enjoy hanging on to that identity. But you'll notice that victims don't have many friends. Their friends are simply tired of hearing "Somebody done me wrong" for the umpteenth time. Really, there is nothing more annoying than a person who won't get over it—eventually—and move on!

Encourage your child to show forgiveness by letting go of grudges. When Ricky doesn't get invited to his friend Jon's birthday party, Ricky can still invite Jon to his. Grudges are such a waste of emotion!

Your child can also demonstrate forgiveness by reconciling friendships. When Joy hasn't talked to her best friend, Angie, for several days because of a fight, help Joy learn the power of being the first to say, "I'm sorry. Will you forgive me?" Help her own her part of the problem, without pointing a finger at Angie.

Mercy

Mercy is a deep caring for other people. It's seeing someone suffering and wanting to ease his or her pain. Mercy, simply put, is compassion in action—when you do something, however small, to try to relieve another's pain.

Encourage your child to show mercy by having a soft spot for others, like sharing her snack with the kid who forgot hers . . . again. Also encourage your child to show a caring heart when someone is hurt physically or emotionally. If a friend is crying, teach your child to get a soft tissue for her and gently rub her back until she feels better. Or if someone has scraped a knee, show your child how to speak comforting words to heal the internal wound while you or another adult tend to the external wound.

Read aloud the story of the Good Samaritan from the Bible.[2] Then contribute to a charity like Compassion International or Samaritan's Purse as a family, or check out ways to volunteer to help the less fortunate in your community.

Friendship

Jesus loved people, no matter how high their social status or how lowly they were. In fact, he was accused by the "popular crowd" of being a friend to "the rejects." Being a friend to all is reaching out to those whom others often reject because of the way they look or the things they do. Teach your child that he should always like the person even if he dislikes the action.

Forgiveness means letting go of a hurtful situation and moving on with your own happiness.
—Amanda Ford

Encourage your child to be a friend to all by treating everyone with respect, accepting others for who they are, and being kind to all, like not excluding a classmate from the pickup game just because he's not very good at sports or doesn't dress like the rest of the kids.

Humility

Having humility is getting rid of the pride, arrogance, and haughtiness that too often creep into our minds when we think we are somehow more beautiful, more talented, or smarter than others.

Encourage your child to show humility by not bragging. If you are good at something, people are going to know; you don't have to keep telling them. Similarly, teach your child to be graceful when accepting compliments. A simple, "Thank you, that's such a nice thing to say" is better than "Yeah, I know I'm good!"

Teach the proverb "Pride comes before a fall,"[3] and talk about what that means in daily life.

Teach your child to be grateful for his good mind (when he points out that "math is a cinch" for him), for her beauty (and emphasize that the true and lasting beauty you love the most is on the inside), and talents (teach your child to say a silent *Thank you* before she plays the piano, or sings, or dances, or runs a race)— to give God praise for his or her body and ability to do all these wonderful things.

Patience

Patience seems like a far-fetched idea in our fast-food world, doesn't it? But it is a wonderful virtue, especially when it comes to being patient with others who are also in progress.

Encourage your child to show patience by being kind to the kid who annoys her at the lunch table. Ask your child to look for two or three good things about this child and try to focus on them.

Better a patient man than a warrior, a man who controls his temper than one who takes a city.
—Proverbs 16:32

Talk about the fact that growing up and maturing takes time. Applaud small efforts toward growth in herself and in her friends.

Another great way to teach your child patience is to encourage her to save up for something she really wants instead of automatically buying it the moment she asks.

Zealousness

Being zealous means to be enthusiastic in everything you do. The Bible says, "Whatever you do, work at it with all your heart."[4] Being zealous is doing your best, whether that is studying for a spelling bee or cleaning your room.

A famous monk named Brother Lawrence wrote a classic little book called *Practicing the Presence of God*, in which he describes how he tried to do even the smallest task with love and meaning and zeal. "I turn my little omelet in the pan for the glory of God," he wrote. I often think of that quote when I'm diapering a baby or rinsing out a sippy cup or picking up toys or making a PB&J for the boys. I try to do all these little things with a reminder that I was called by God to care for the needs of small children. What a difference it makes when I remember to have this mind-set. Look out—I can be one zealous nanny!

Encourage your child to be zealous by working diligently in school. Be sure that you and your spouse show pride and enthusiasm over small victories and little tasks your child has done well.

Nanny Tip

Encourage your children to set goals for themselves, and work with them toward accomplishing those goals. Help them write down a goal and make it very clear. Then write down the steps it will take for them to meet that goal. This process teaches organization, motivation, patience, and perseverance.

You can also help your child become zealous by having a cause. Encourage your child to come up with something she cares for, and she'll develop a passion for it that will result in a determination to make a difference.

Help your child find meaning in the mundane by talking about ways to make daily tasks more fun or purposeful. In fact, you might list all the activities, big and small, that your child has to do. Then talk about how you can upsize the fun factor or find more creative ways to do life's tasks. For example, maybe you can play the theme song from *Rocky* while he cleans his room, boxer-in-training style, with gusto. Maybe you can come up with a game that makes taking out the trash fun, like timing your child to see how fast he can get it to the curb and run back in the house. Doing dishes while listening to an audiobook makes cleanup a breeze, and it's informative too!

Self-Discipline

It's never too early to encourage your children to have a healthy sense of self-discipline. You can foster your child's ability to be independent by teaching him age-appropriate simple living skills, which include how to wash clothes, how to iron a shirt well, how to cook a pot roast, how to set a table correctly, how to write a check or balance a checkbook, how to check the oil in the car (yes, even before they are driving), and how to handle a variety of emergencies.

Encourage your child to be self-disciplined with her time by putting an alarm clock in her room and having her set the alarm each night. You can also buy her a day planner, just like the grown-ups have. Show her how to use it for homework assignments, school practices, group and family functions, planning and goal setting, and keeping all her important information in one place.

Teach your child the nutritional value of food and have him help you make great recipes that use healthful ingredients. Savor food slowly. Emphasize the joy and fun of and need for movement to stay in shape and relieve stress—all of these things will contribute to self-discipline for eating well and staying fit.

God Is Always with You

Although I'm not sure we can classify this as a virtue, I love to teach kids the simple but profound truth that they never have to be alone, because God goes with them everywhere! Not only that, but they can talk to Him in prayer and He'll listen anytime, day or night, and anywhere, whether they are at home, school, or play.

I don't ever promise a child that God will answer his prayers the way he wants them answered, but I do promise that God can give him a peaceful feeling inside when he gets anxious or scared. If he feels rejected, I tell him that he can be sure of God's love—God will never turn His back on anyone. Never ever. Now that is good news for kids of all ages!

Scene 14: Take 2
At the School Lunch Table

DARLENE. I am so hungry. I forgot to eat breakfast and didn't bring my lunch.

KENDALL. Well, go buy something.

DARLENE. Yeah, of all days, I forgot my backpack on the bus.

KENDALL, *enjoying her homemade lunch.* What a bummer, huh? I'll have to help
  you think of a better morning system so you don't forget things.

(Both girls chuckle.)

KENDALL. Here is half my sandwich, and I'll share my drink—just leave
  me a sip.

DARLENE. I called my mom to ask her to bring me something, but she's not
  at her desk at work. So thanks, I really, really love ya for it.

KENDALL. Wow. I wish I had some more money so we could both get
  dessert, but I only have enough for one ice cream sandwich, so we'll
  have to half it.

DARLENE. I knew there was a reason you're my best friend!

KENDALL. Thank my mom; she's the one who taught me how to be a good
  friend!

Nanny to the Rescue Again!
Recap

What made Kendall a good friend?

1. *She was compassionate.* She knew her friend was hungry and did something to help.
2. *She showed mercy.* She didn't have to share her lunch, but she did.
3. *She gave grace.* Her friend was a forgetful person, but she loved her anyway.
4. *She was helpful.* She offered to help her friend devise a system to stay organized in the morning.
5. *She was disciplined.* She shared her dessert, even though she wanted it all—what kid doesn't!
6. *She was obedient.* Her mom taught her how to behave, and she followed through—even when her mom wasn't there to see.

BACKTALK AND OTHER UNWANTED GIFTS FROM A TO Z

If you have a son between the ages of six and twelve, by now you've probably discovered that nothing makes a grade-school boy as gleeful as gross humor. Once they learn to make disgusting noises with their hands cupped under their armpits, it is a downhill slide from there. You may have also found out that your social butterfly daughter has distributed family secrets, with exaggeration for dramatic effect, to her Girl Scout troop. Bathroom humor can cause children to laugh so hard that they may literally wet their pants. They can tell corny, nonstop knock-knock jokes to your relatives until even their grandmother, who thinks all her grandchildren are perfect, groans for relief.

In short, there's an awful lot of social awkwardness during the gangly grade-school years. If there were a music CD to describe this stage, it might be called *Songs to Embarrass Your Parents*.

Here's a case in point from my own nanny files. Austin's class had earned a special theme party for doing consistent good work and behavior. The kids voted on a pajama movie party, and sure enough, on the big day all the students showed up in their jammies, with their sleeping bags in tow. I showed up in my bathrobe and slippers, over my clothes, along with a few other class moms. Enter a dad who had also volunteered to help with this event. When he showed up in his jammies—lounge pants and a T-shirt—his son looked shocked and yelled, "Dad, why are you wearing that outfit? You sleep naked!" As his dad turned bright red, we all had a great laugh. So much for family privacy.

I remember an encounter with a first-grade diva on my first babysitting assignment with a new family. As soon as her parents had slipped out the door, she put one hand on her hip and began chewing her gum loudly, all the while assuring me, "My brother is really annoying. Thank goodness, I am not like that at all."

The first time my young charge snapped a "Whatever!" at me, my jaw dropped as I wondered what happened to *my* kid. And then there was the first time I overheard a made-up song by a proud and loud child that carefully (and artfully) described every detail of his latest trip to the bathroom.

The unwanted gifts of school-age children may frustrate and annoy you now, but rest assured, years—and sometimes just a few moments or days—later, the awkward scenarios will replay through your mind, leaving you with funny memories that turn into gifts of their own.

Here is my personal ABC "problemossary" of annoying and unwanted gifts that I have been given over the years—and of course, some nanny tips and tricks to nip them in the bud before they get too out of hand.

Attitude

"Lose the 'tude." I like that phrase because it reminds a child (and me!) that attitudes and behaviors can be changed, and in fairly short order—if you are motivated.

Here's my method for helping a child in desperate need of an attitude adjustment. First, I try to get to the root of what is causing the attitude. Bad day? Wrong side of the bed? Need a nap?

Then I try to use humor and reverse psychology if it is appropriate. "I dare you not to smile. This is a terrible, horrible, no good, very bad day, and I sure don't want to see you smile or laugh. OK?" For young kids especially, this is almost a surefire attitude changer, because they simply can't keep from grinning.

I will ask them if there's anything they need that I can give them that can help them feel better. But I also emphasize, "It is OK to be sad. It is OK to be mad. But there is *never* an excuse for being rude. Everybody can be nice and polite, even if they are upset."

Teach them not to "kick the dog." Say, "Once there was this man who would get so mad about his job. And every day he'd come home and kick the dog so he'd feel better." Let them respond to the unfairness of the story. Then say, "Sometimes when you are angry about something at school or just in a bad mood, I feel like the dog that got kicked for no reason."

Assure them that we all have low moods and sad days, and we are affected by everything from lack of sun to lack of exercise to situations that are sad or confusing. "It's OK to cry. It is OK to talk through a problem. It just isn't OK to be ugly to other people." Then model this. Tell your kids, "I don't know why, but I'm just feeling blue, and I don't want to take my bad feelings out on you. I need to go cheer myself up by having a cup of tea and reading a book on the porch. After I have a bit of alone time, I'll be much better. Would you be extra understanding with my feelings for the next hour or so? I need some TLC so I can get back to the happy me!"

Backtalk

"Yeah, whatever," your child says nonchalantly as her eyes roll and her hips swing to one side. Do I really need to define *backtalk*? Most parents (and nannies) have built-in backtalk radars. You know it when you hear it. The first time backtalk rears its ugly head, it is important to send it packing immediately.

Because I have received this gift one too many times over the years of working with kids, the "no backtalk" rule is always written in the family code. When you take the proactive approach and set the standard from the beginning, you are less likely to encounter backtalk on any sort of regular basis. When I occasionally do encounter it, I point it out to my charge in a calm but firm manner as soon as I hear or see it. "Excuse me, Austin, but that was backtalk I just heard coming out of that precious mouth of yours. That tone of voice was not OK. Can you try again?" I believe in giving children an immediate chance at a "do-over"—because if they can learn to catch and correct their own words, the lesson is over and we can go on our polite and merry little way. If, however, I get an argument in return or a continued pattern of disrespect or even a sarcastic, drawn-out, or insincere "Sorry," then a consequence gets imposed—usually a time-out or the loss of a privilege.

Sometimes children say rude things in a sincere attempt to be funny or cool. If you suspect this may be the case, you can ask, "Did you realize that statement could have really hurt my feelings? Why did you say it?" Give them a chance to clear the air. They sincerely could be repeating something they heard on a playground that got a laugh among peers and have no clue that it is inappropriate.

A friend told me that when she was in third grade, she heard a joke at school and had no idea what it meant. But she noted that it got a good laugh, so she came home and proudly repeated it to her mother's bridge club. She had no idea she'd just told the ladies an off-color story. Thankfully, her mom handled it well, knowing her daughter was truly innocent in her "sharing." And to this day, when they remember the incident, they both get the giggles.

Cuss Words

We were enjoying a little TV time one evening, cheering on our favorite football team together. Suddenly our happy family reverie was interrupted by a very loud and clear cuss word coming from the mouth of a six-year-old who was unhappy with the play of the opposing team.

I pushed the mute button immediately (if only there were remote-control mute buttons that we could use with our kids!) and then sent an arsenal of questions his direction. "What did you just say? Do you know what that word even means? Where did you hear that word? Why would you say it?"

Well, he'd overheard some men watching a game at a sports-themed family restaurant. He was just mimicking what he'd seen and heard in a moment of sports passion, truly thinking this is the way a real sports fan shows strong emotion. Kids are like sponges and absorb most everything they see and hear. This includes things from adults, television, movies, video games, computer games, and their peers.

Because I know that the influence I have on the children in my care is strong, I am always careful to model appropriate language. I do not want them repeating a slip of the tongue back to me someday and saying, "We heard you say that word when you got mad!" Setting a good example by using only the language that you wish your child to use is the best preventative measure you can take to keep your child from swearing.

When you do mess up, as we all do, it's important to point it out and apologize. Sometimes I think I may have overemphasized the point. To this day, if the boys (first graders now) hear me say the word *stupid* as I'm talking on the phone to a friend, they respond in stereo, "Shell! We don't use that word. Remember?" I have to respond with a sincere, "Oops, you guys are right. I'm sorry."

You might also give your kids some appropriate, funny, inoffensive words to yell when they are angry or highly involved in a football game. One mother taught her kids to say, "Fiddlesticks!" when they bumped their head or stubbed their toe. See how creative you and your kids can be: "Fizzwhizit! Pooberscoot! Gallywagger!" The upside of making up your own funny family words is that you can quickly turn anger into laughter.

Dinner Disasters

"I'm not eating that." Just recently, a classmate of my charges and his family were over for dinner. I had made some tortellini and pesto, as well as a mac and cheese dish with beef. (OK, I confess: it was Hamburger Helper.) My charges sat and ate happily, chatting away, while their friend insisted he was not eating what he was served, pushed his plate away, spilled his milk, and began to whine that he was hungry.

My charges looked at me, surprised at this kid's behavior, and said, "Shell, doesn't he know this is not a restaurant and you don't always get just what you want?" Then they told the friend how it's important to eat what is provided "because it is healthy for your body." Then they laid on the guilt. "And some kids have no food at all." Then they lectured. "And it is rude to not at least try something when at a guest's house, even if it's new."

The friend's mom, who was sitting nearby, had a different philosophy and agreed to take Mr. Picky home and make his dinner to her child's specifications. The expressions on the faces of my charges were priceless. Every cell of their bodies were saying, "You gotta be *kidding* me!"

Now, I don't intentionally serve the boys foods they don't like, though naturally, at times they may have preferred something different. But they are sure of the standards set in our home and know what is expected of them at the dinner table. In turn, I know they have learned a fabulous lesson in how to behave when they are guests at someone else's home—a lesson that will go with them for a lifetime.

It is important that dinner be pleasant. It's a time for family sharing and socializing, not arguing and bickering. (Upset people at mealtime cause upset tummies.) We share things about our day and listen to what others have to say. We clean up our own dishes, and at least in our home, not every night is a dessert night. I don't insist that the kids eat everything on their plates, but I do remind them that they need to pay attention and eat their fill because I won't be serving supper again in an hour.

Entitlement

"Get me this. I deserve that." Dealing with a sense of entitlement is a common struggle for today's parents. Some children feel the world constantly owes them something, without their having to work, earn, or engage in any responsibility to make what they want come into their possession.

Some kids from affluence have a Richie Rich syndrome (remember that cartoon?). They are used to having hired help around the house, and they come to believe they are miniature bosses of their own private universes. One time, I was caring for a ten-year-old from an affluent family, and she insisted it was my job to pick up her dirty underwear because she was my boss. Needless to say, I corrected her on the particulars of my job description.

But acting like a spoiled brat isn't limited to the rich. Sometimes children of poverty feel that they deserve special treatment because of their status. Many times, those in a low-income family system have learned to expect others (the government, school, church) to give them what might have been easily earned.

A sense of entitlement knows no race, no socioeconomic boundaries, and no educational differences. No matter what the race or economic status of your child, a sense of entitlement will ruin his life. So pay attention to attitudes of "The world owes me something," and do all you can to help your children wake up to life's reality. As the Bible says, "He who does not work shall not eat."[1] Now this doesn't mean we shouldn't help one another. But each person should contribute whatever he is able to do, to pay his own way in life.

Very little in this life builds a person's self-esteem like a job well done and a privilege or possession earned. Here are some tips to help avoid the unwanted gift of entitlement in your child.

Kids should be taught to pick up their plate, take it to the sink, rinse it, and put it in the dishwasher after meals. (Or at the minimum, put it in the sink.) He eats; he cleans. Fact of life.

When your child expresses a desire of a major purchase like expensive name-brand tennis shoes, you can offer to contribute the money equal to a pair of off-brand shoes and have your child pay for or earn (with extra "jobs") the rest of the money for his Air Jordans.

Some parents have an overwhelming desire to make certain their child never goes without, which results in a child never experiencing postponed satisfaction. Perhaps you came from true poverty and are overcompensating in an unbalanced way. It is good for every child to experience patience, waiting, and making do without a coveted toy or piece of clothing. Teens who don't learn this valuable lesson are soon running up huge credit-card bills as soon as they get their first card.

When your child wants the latest "in" item, sit down with a pen and piece of paper first. Ask questions like, "Is there a way to make this ourselves in order to save money? Can we look for the same item at a bargain store or online? How long will it take you to save for it if you mow lawns every Saturday? Is there a less expensive version that would give you just as much pleasure and fun?" You don't always have to say no to a child's request. It might be wiser to say, "How could you get that item yourself?" Working out compromises, such as going "halfsies" on items, and setting a budget for their school clothing (but letting them pick out what they want within that set budget) empower your children with the opportunity to exercise their budget.

My charges went through a phase where they began to feel entitled to a dessert every night after dinner. When I saw that it became an assumption and expectation, I put a stop to it. They no longer got dessert on a regular basis, and if they asked for it, they wouldn't get it for two nights in a row. When they got dessert on an unpredictable basis, they quickly stopped taking it for granted and appreciated the special treats that they were occasionally allowed to indulge in.

The reality of "the kid who has it all" is that that the kid who has it all really doesn't. They don't understand how to process "No" or "Not now" in the real world, and they don't have the skills needed to handle the difficult feelings that they may face. Since they are used to always getting, they don't learn how to be in give-and-take relationships, which makes developing healthy friendships difficult.

Forgetfulness

"I didn't know. I just forgot." Do you ever feel like your child would forget his own head if it wasn't attached to his body? He forgot his gym clothes; she can't find her lunch box. He has no idea where he put his homework assignment that is due in twenty minutes, and she can't find her mittens!

Forgetfulness in school-age children can be quite frustrating, because sometimes it is hard to discern between true forgetfulness and sheer irresponsibility. During the grade-school years, most healthy children naturally develop an increasing sense of responsibility. Schoolwork loads increase, demands for remembering items for extracurricular activities come into play, and daily home life has now brought a new level of expectations for your child. Sometimes the responsibilities that pile up with growing up can be overwhelming. Here are a few ways to help make your child a "rememberer."

Help your child be responsible for her belongings by providing an organized place for everything. In our home, we have a special shelf in the kitchen for library books, and the kids know that on library day the books will be there because that's where they belong. Their backpacks get packed and left by the back door each evening and are ready for pickup on the way out the door in the morning. There is a place for everything, which eliminates the morning search-and-rescue missions.

If your child seems to forget things regularly because he is preoccupied or just has a hard time remembering things, put a checklist by the door, listing all the items he needs for school each day. Backpack, check. Lunch, check. Shin pads, check. Homework, check.

Chore charts are another way to help kids keep track of what they've done and what they still need to do around the house. Dirty laundry away, check. Room cleaned up, check. Dog fed, check. (Can you tell that I love checking off lists?)

If there's a pattern, look deeper. A child who seems to forget his lunch or homework regularly could be masking another problem. Ask him to tell you about lunchtime. Ask him if he understands his homework assignments. You may be surprised to learn that he is isn't coming home with a clear understanding of his assignments, so he just "forgets" to do them. Or perhaps someone is bullying him for his lunch so he "forgets" to bring it rather than seek help from you or a teacher.

When your child fails to take on a responsibility that was clearly defined, you can use consequences to get him back on track. Forgot your lunch? The first time or two, you may take him his lunch. But he may need to suffer a natural consequence—not eating—for one lunch period so his memory will kick into gear. "Didn't clean your room? Sorry, can't play outside until it's done!" Logical consequences can really help jog your memory!

Greed

"I don't have enough shoes! I need one in every color!" You're not sure if the TV is tuned to *Desperate Housewives* or if you are overhearing the conversations of ten-year-old girls in your daughter's bedroom.

"Get me," "I want to have," "I need," "Buy me," "I'll die if I don't get that," and "I'll hate you if you don't" are all opening lines in the daily drama of a child who is or wants to be overindulged. When these requests are coupled with persistence, pleases, pity, and promises, it's often hard for a parent to say no. "Mom, can I *please* have that new computer game? It will really help with my fine motor skills. I promise I'll behave and only play it one hour a day. Don't you want me to be as smart as John? He just got the game yesterday." Makes it hard to argue. Or you simply get worn down.

One of the best ways to cure greed is to take an active role in giving to others. Teach your kids the value and meaning behind the truth that it is better to give than receive. When I was leaving for Africa on a missionary trip last summer, Fraser insisted I take some DVDs for the kids at the orphanage. He had a really hard time processing the fact that these children had no TV, and certainly no VCRs or DVD players. Once he processed it, the truth hit him hard.

One year later, every time he goes to watch a movie, he remembers and says, "I'm lucky. Some kids don't have DVDs." Coming to grips with the reality that others don't always have what we have can change a child's outlook and increase his gratitude for all the blessings and riches (not just monetary in value) around him. Once Fraser realized he had things that others didn't, he wanted to change it. His heart was touched by the needs of starving children who had no mom or dad.

It's a great idea for a family to support an underprivileged child or to keep a piggy bank going to give to a worthy cause. We all need reminders of how truly wealthy most Americans are compared to those in Third World countries. Even some of the poorest Americans would be among the wealthy in parts of India or Africa.

Schools and communities pull together to raise money for victims of natural disasters, toys for children at Christmas, and food for families at Thanksgiving.

Take an active role in participating in these activities. My charges have worked lemonade stands, saved their pennies, and donated used and new toys in the effort to help others who are less fortunate. I encourage you to make giving to and helping others part of your year-round routine. As a family, you can sponsor a child, take part in community service, or find many other ways to help those who are less fortunate. Often kids will come up with their own ideas of how to help.

One birthday, Fraser was so excited that he got two of the same gifts. He was truly thrilled he'd be able to give one to a child who was less fortunate. I love when Austin decides to clean out his toy bins just because he thinks he has too many Bionicles and some children have none, so it may be nice to give them to others. He boxes them up and we drop them off together.

Hardheadedness

"Your shirt is blue, Mom, not aquamarine." "Actually, Sam, aquamarine is a shade of blue." "No, blue is blue, aquamarine is aquamarine." Ugh, the frustration when you are trying to teach a child something new, but he simply won't listen. He knows it all and will argue until he is literally blue (or should I say "aquamarine"?) in the face, rather than admit that he actually may be wrong.

Or when your child wants to swim in the deep end of the pool alone, and you reply, "You can't swim in the deep end yet because there is no lifeguard on duty and it's not safe." It just doesn't process. He knows how to swim, he wants to swim, so why can't he? His reasoning must be right; others are wrong, end of story. Not every child is this stubborn, but if you are a mother of several kids, you probably have one. Every teacher gets at least one or two hardheaded students.

When I've dealt with a hardheaded child (I'm sure the way my mom dealt with me), I've found it helps to begin by communicating what is going to happen in an even, nonemotional tone. "Listen, we can't swim now because the lifeguard isn't here. We will swim as soon as she arrives." Acknowledge his feelings. "I know that waiting stinks, but we have no other choice." Don't give in to the repeated attempts to get you to change your mind. Silence in this stage can be your friend. Refuse to discuss the topic again. If arguing continues, you can either ride it out or leave the area and take away the privilege. If you choose to give the "lose the privilege" warning, only issue it if you are ready to follow through. Say, "You need to pull yourself together, or we won't swim at all"—and be prepared to leave the pool if the attitude continues.

Instant Gratification

"Can't you use your credit card?" came spurting out of the mouth of an eight-year-old child when I told her we couldn't get ice cream because I didn't have any money with me.

In today's fast-food, drive-through society, children often have no concept of what's behind the plastic or the daily deliveries from UPS. In an age when Internet shopping is on the increase, ATM machines are located at every corner, and debit- and credit-card machines are even found in Dunkin' Donuts, the concept of cash has almost gone the way of the dinosaur.

Have you heard of the famous Stanford marshmallow study? Researchers gave a set of four-year-old kids a choice: have one marshmallow now, or wait fifteen minutes and have two marshmallows. Interestingly, they interviewed those same kids ten years later, and those who had chosen to wait for the two marshmallows scored an average of 210 points higher on their SAT scores. But that was only the tip of the iceberg. "The resisters were more positive, self-motivating, persistent in the face of difficulties, and able to delay gratification in pursuit of their goals. They had the habits of successful people which resulted in more successful marriages, higher incomes, greater career satisfaction, better health, and more fulfilling lives than most of the population."[2]

In contrast, "those having grabbed the marshmallow were more troubled, stubborn and indecisive, mistrustful, less self-confident, and still could not put off gratification. They had trouble subordinating immediate impulses to achieve long-range goals. When it was time to study for the big test, they tended to get distracted into doing activities that brought instant gratification. This impulse followed them throughout their lives and resulted in unsuccessful marriages, low job satisfaction and income, bad health, and frustrating lives."[3]

Based on this study and others, researchers now believe that being able to tolerate delayed gratification plays a significant role in emotional intelligence, one of the top indicators for a successful and happy life. So do *not* feel guilty when you require that your child wait and work for a longed-for reward. You are teaching her how to tolerate small, temporary discomfort and to self-soothe in order to hold out for a greater reward later on—and giving her a gift that will keep on giving for the rest of her life.

Jealousy

"You love her more; she's your favorite." With siblings and especially twins, jealousy is a gift that keeps on giving, and giving, and giving. It's a never-ending struggle to make sure everyone knows they are special and loved.

I strongly recommend reading *The Five Love Languages of Children* by Gary Chapman.[4] It gives great insight into how different people send and receive love and will help you determine how best your child perceives love. In his book, Chapman breaks down the five major categories that communicate love to people.

If your love language is . . .	You feel loved when . . .
Words of Affirmation	someone says uplifting or encouraging words to you
Receiving Gifts	someone gives you a gift
Quality Time	someone spends time with you
Acts of Service	someone helps you out
Physical Touch	someone shows you affection

Treat each child as a unique individual. Identify their strengths and their weaknesses, and provide ways for them to use their strengths. If one child loves to draw, sign her up for art class where she has a chance to succeed in something she loves.

If the other loves sports, don't make him take the art class, but get him on the baseball team.

End the comparisons. "Why can't you just do it like your sister?" may seem like an innocent comment, but it has the potential to engage siblings in lifelong struggles. Resentments and grudges are built on comments like these, which are often interpreted as, "You love her more than me." Keeping siblings in separate classes or on separate sports teams may take a bit of extra effort, but it just may be worth it.

Spend alone time with each child. Some of my best memories are when we had the kids' schedule arranged so that every other day, one would come home from school early and the other would stay late in extended kindergarten. We loved having the one-on-one time with each other. I could focus my attention on Austin alone, or Fraser alone, and do exactly what each boy wanted for the afternoon. We could play *Battleship* without interruption. We could read together without having to stop to make sure the other saw the pictures. We enjoyed each other's undivided attention. Now they are a bit older and the school schedule isn't as flexible, so I arrange playdates on alternative days or have only one child have a friend over so I can play with the other. It's a real treat for all of us. I remember reading that Susanna Wesley, respected mother of John and Charles Wesley and seventeen other children, made it a priority to spend some time alone with each child each week. What a great example for all of us.

Set clear boundaries with the kids. Don't allow siblings to tease each other when one of them asks the other to stop. If a child needs privacy or alone time from his sibling, respect that. And if the kids feel like playing alone instead of together, it is OK. Encourage your children always to treat others (and their possessions) the way that they wish to be treated.

Kissing Up

It's been said that flattery will get you everywhere. It especially works well when kids use it to try to get out of trouble. The other day I heard a child say, "Mom, I'm sorry. You are the best, and you know I would never want to make you mad because you are such a pretty mama." The mom immediately reduced the disciplinary sentence from a thirty-minute time-out to an "OK, give me a hug and go play." Remember Eddie Haskell from *Leave It to Beaver*? "You look so lovely today, Mrs. Cleaver," he'd say. Then the moment her back was turned, he'd be rude to the Beav or cook up some naughty scheme. Another thing some siblings love to do is to point out how bad their sibling is behaving but ask you to take note of their angelic behavior.

The best way to deal with a child who is trying to charm his way out of trouble (or put others in a bad light so he'll look better) is to ignore it or make sure you don't treat him any differently. Make it clear to your children that flattery won't change the rules. Disparaging others to make yourself look better isn't going to get you any points. In fact, it is good to say, "You know, your little brother's behavior is between him and me. You don't need to point out any flaws, as I'm sure you wouldn't want him to do the same to you when you've misbehaved."

Lying

"I didn't do it. It wasn't me." If kids came with directions, one of the disclaimers would read: "Caution: this child will eventually tell a lie." All kids tell lies, and it seems to peak around ages five to seven, when they can tell you the most outlandish tales with the straightest of faces. "We had a lion come over for dinner last night, and I got to pet it, and it even slept in my bed! But it snored so much it kept me awake."

There are several types of lies. The most innocent of all is the exaggerations of young children with vivid imaginations. Like the scenario above, these fantastic tales are so harmless, they can barely be defined as lies. They are the tall tales and fantasy fables commonly told by younger children. By age seven or eight, these wild stories begin to cease, as a child becomes aware of the difference between fantasy and reality. Until this age, children are life's greatest exaggerators. "I saw a snake! It was twelve feet long and its fangs were two feet long!" Most likely, the child did indeed see a snake, just not one as big and exciting as he described.

One of the most common reasons that children tell an actual lie—a complete mistruth—is in an attempt to divert blame or get out of trouble. Younger kids often blame things on their imaginary friends, but older kids will tell an outright lie to cover up the truth in hopes of avoiding the consequence. By age ten, most children can concretely distinguish between right and wrong and should be held accountable for their actions.

Compulsive lying is of the most concern. Serious, continuous patterns of intentional deceit need to be addressed firmly and consistently. Clear expectations need to be defined, and consequences need to be imposed. When your child claims to have completed his homework each night and you find out he hasn't been doing it, the consequence should be no fun and games after school until homework is done and you've checked it. When he says he wasn't playing ball in the house as the ball flies through the air and breaks your favorite vase, he loses the privilege of going to baseball practice that day. When the lies become repetitive and predictable, you need to buckle down and be consistent in enforcing consequences.

The following will help you instill the importance of truth in your child:

- *Model good behavior.* Say what you mean, and mean what you say.
- *Don't lie to your child.* Maybe you don't remember, but a booster shot actually does hurt!
- *Don't encourage your children to lie.* Don't ask him to tell the waitress that he is ten so he can eat off the children's menu. Don't say, "If Katherine calls, tell her I'm not here."
- *Be clear.* Don't distinguish between a white lie and a black lie—a lie is a lie.
- *When your child tells the truth when he easily could have lied, praise him for it.* "I'm proud you chose to tell the truth. I know it wasn't easy." One of Susanna Wesley's rules for raising her children included, "Never punish a child when he tells the truth and sincerely confesses a sin or a mistake."
- *Love the child; hate the lie.* Always address the behavior, not the child. "I love you. I don't like when you tell lies."

- *Don't set your child up to lie.* If you know the answer to the question, don't ask. Asking, "Did you eat the last cookie?" when you see the crumbs all over his mouth gets you nowhere. Instead, acknowledge the facts and allow him to take part in the problem solving. "It looks like you ate the last cookie even though I asked you not to. What should we do about it?"
- *Always encourage truth telling.* Remind your child that you'd always rather hear the truth. "I may be disappointed, but I want to know the truth, because I'd be more disappointed if I knew you lied."

When face-to face with a lying child, I have found success in talking about the behavior that prompted the lie, addressing why lying made it worse (because now I am disappointed not only with the behavior but also with the lie), and allowing the child to choose a consequence that he finds reasonable. Most often, the child selects a much tougher consequence than I would have imposed.

I tell the child that I am not mad or sad, but "I am disappointed that you had a choice to tell the truth or a lie and you chose to tell the lie. Next time, I believe you can choose better, OK?"

Getting angry or yelling at your child after she has admitted the lie and told the truth isn't going to teach her the value of truth telling but will most likely have the opposite effect. The child will be so scared to tell the truth the next time around, she will avoid it at all costs. Talking through the importance of being honest and allowing her to help solve the problem by selecting a consequence teaches rather than tortures.

Mocking

"Please clean your room."

"Please clean your room."

"I'm serious."

"I'm serious."

Add a bad attitude, a high-pitched voice, and a mean streak, and you've got a very irritating mini-me in your house. Mocking—poking fun by copying what someone is saying or mimicking what one is doing—is annoying, to say the least.

At first glance it may seem funny, but the digs go deep quickly. Mocking is a belittling behavior, meant to put another person down so you can get the emotional upper hand. Kids will often mock their teachers to get attention or to be the class clown. The teacher will say something and turn around to write on the chalkboard, and self-appointed Bozo will seize the opportunity to stand up at his desk and begin to copy what she is doing. The kids "won" and the class laughed, but a teacher was treated disrespectfully.

Mocking is a form of ridicule, and even if it gets a laugh, it is unkind. We have a rule that unkind behavior is not acceptable. When I ask my charges to "get ready for a shower" and they repeat my words in a snippy, mocking tone of voice, they immediately know what to expect—a firm look from me and a "take five" (time-out) as they head to their "thinking chair" to contemplate their inappropriate behavior.

Negativity

"No one likes me. I can't do anything right. I hate snow! I hate sunshine! I hate rain! I don't like school. I don't like peas. I don't like that TV show. I don't like your shirt." This is the gift of never-ending negativity, also known as a permanent bad mood. Like adults, kids often have mood swings, and if you observe carefully, you can almost predict them. With most kids, a hungry child equals a miserable one. A tired child equals an irritable one. You can keep the swing balanced if you are proactive by providing your child with a structured lifestyle. Healthy food and a good night's sleep go a long way in preventing misery.

When my charge enters the negative zone, I try to figure out what's bothering him by asking open-ended questions. "Tell me about school," I might say. Oftentimes a social interaction between a classmate is enough to put a dent in his entire day. I always try to acknowledge and validate his feelings, but I put a limit on ways in which his feelings are allowed to be expressed. "I understand you are feeling really upset about what happened in school. I'd be upset, too, but you can't hit your brother because you are mad at your school friend." If he doesn't respond and the negative behavior increases, I give him a firm warning. "Enough of the behavior. You can stay and play properly, or you can go to your room. I don't want to hear another negative comment or see another negative behavior related to that topic. You've had time to vent and talk about it—now you are just rolling around in it. Time to get out of the mud and move on, buddy."

If it appears he is just in a bad mood and nothing significant has caused it, I'll ignore the mood, but not the child. I'll go on with things as usual and encourage him to take part. Everyone is entitled to have a bad day, but recently my charge taught me something new. He said, "Shell, I don't have bad days; I just have bad moments." I loved it. And he's right: most of us just have a few low moments in an otherwise pretty great day. If you model positive attitudes and behaviors and praise your child when he follows suit, his bad days will turn into moments.

Although she gets a bad rap, sometimes I highly recommend reading the classic book *Pollyanna* or watching the movie. Get a flip calendar with positive messages to start each day, read an uplifting quote on the way to school each morning, or keep a family blessings journal and have everyone record all the good things that happen. The default mode of the human mind is often negative, so we have to be proactive in filling our minds with positive thoughts.

Obnoxious Behavior

"Move out of the way!" a child says to a schoolmate on the bus as she forces her way into a full seat. Or perhaps you found out that your son decided to "moon" the elderly neighbor from his window, just for laughs. I once corrected a child for throwing rocks at my charges, and he "shot me the bird"—and I don't mean that he threw a robin my direction.

When your child displays obnoxious behavior, point out the behavior and demand that it stop because it is unacceptable: "Stop yelling in your brother's face. That is not acceptable." If he doesn't stop, send him to time-out and have him do something during this time to constructively redirect his thoughts and behavior.

You might have him read a paragraph or two on valuing others and report to you what he read, or maybe have him memorize a verse like, "Be kind and compassionate to one another, forgiving each other."[5] If he stops the behavior, praise him for his obedience and encourage him to apologize to his sibling. Catch him being good, and reinforce the behavior you do like.

Eliminating obnoxious behavior in the early years is a great service to your child. Too often we see grown men getting arrested at their children's sporting events as a result of screaming obscenities and exhibiting other unruly behavior. They look, quite honestly, like giant toddlers having a tantrum, and one begins to wonder if they had a mom or dad or caregiver who ignored their obnoxious behavior, allowing it to escalate over the years. Remind your child that no one wants to be friends with someone who is constantly bossy, rude, and offensive.

Potty Mouth

We were driving home from school, and three little boys began singing a little ditty about "poop," and they were laughing so hard that they could hardly catch their breath. Me? I didn't know whether to laugh or cry. The days I dreaded of bathroom humor had begun. And honestly, do boys ever completely outgrow this? Lots of grown men think potty humor is simply hilarious. I am trying to understand, but I just don't get it.

Passing gas (the real and the artificially simulated noises), burping (the natural and forced kind), calling someone a "poop head," and making references to food looking like something gross are all normal behaviors in the world of elementary-school boys.

I've told my charges that they can talk about their bodies and their functions all they want—in the bathroom with the door closed. I've taught them that some people don't like to hear about their bodies and what they are doing, and we need to respect that. Some people laugh, but some get queasy—so it is best not to over-share information that not everyone wants to hear.

I've also taught them that it is OK to laugh at the funny noises that their bodies make or to make up their own funny bathroom stories, but they aren't to be shared in public. There's "family humor," and then there's "public humor." Now, I'm sure when the boys are with a group of boys their own age, there is also "guy humor." I'm optimistic but not naive. Boys *will* be boys.

This isn't really a major disciplinary category—all it usually takes is a raised eyebrow and saying, "Enough!" in my firmest nanny voice. If the boys can't stop the giggles over poopy jokes, I just send them to the bathroom and tell them to come out when they are finished with their gross jokes and nonstop peals of laughter. "You guys can tell poopy jokes with the door closed, but I'm cooking supper and I don't want to hear it, thank you very much."

Questioning

"Who, what, when, where, why?" rings out loud and clear when I'm on the phone attempting to schedule an outing with friends. "Who are you talking to? What are we doing? Where are we going? When are we going? Why are we going? Do we have to go?" And then there is the infamous "Are we there yet?" Not to mention all the curious questions: "Why is the sky blue? Why did God make bugs with stingers? What is the biggest fish in the ocean?"

Kids come complete with questions. Often they ask questions out of curiosity; it is the way they learn. In this case, answer them as honestly as you can, or promise to try to find out the answers. If you have a kid who is constantly chitchatting, thinking, and asking questions like, "How do they make Dr. Pepper? Why is the moon sometimes yellow and sometimes white?" You may wish you were Einstein with the patience of Mother Teresa. As soon as your Curious George can write, buy him a blank journal and call it his Question Book. Have him write down all his questions about the world, life, and anything else that is buzzing around in his noggin. Then one afternoon, spend some time at the library or with an encyclopedia or do some Internet searches and play "Find That Answer!" together. There are some great books on the market that are simply page after page of answers to random but interesting questions.

Children need to learn to save their questions for an appropriate time to ask them. This will be true for them throughout their lives, especially in school when they have to wait their turn to talk to the teacher. By jotting down their questions, they won't forget them. Also, they need to learn where to find answers to their questions outside of asking you or their teacher. Show them how to find information at the library or on the Internet.

Rumor Spreading

"I heard that Molly cheated on her test." "Did you hear that if we don't behave in Mrs. Kayright's class today, we are all going to get detention?" Rumors are unverified information spread from person to person. Like the old game of telephone, each time the information is shared, it is altered a bit, and the final "story" is usually a far cry from the original information.

Slander is a type of rumor that is set out to personally hurt someone. "Meghan cheats on her spelling tests, so stay away from her or she'll copy you!" These negative rumors being spread about the child may cause her to be an outcast in the classroom.

Some people spread rumors to get attention, to get back at someone, to feel better about themselves, or just because they are bored. Regardless of the type of rumor or reasoning behind it, a "no tolerance" policy for gossip should be in effect in your home. It is fun, in a voyeuristic way, to talk about other people's pain and problems. (If it weren't, the *National Enquirer* would be out of business.) The reason we are interested in the downfall of others is that it somehow makes us feel that we are better. By stepping on others, people feel much taller. But if you or your child has ever been the subject of a rumor, you know that it hurts. No one enjoys getting a verbal slap in the face by lots of people at once. That's what a rumor feels like—whether the information is true or not.

Encourage your children not to take part in spreading rumors. When they hear something bad about someone else, encourage them not to be part of the vicious circle. Help them back off from the gossip grapevine by saying something like, "I wouldn't want other people talking badly about me, even if I did make a mistake."

When your child is the subject of the rumor, encourage her to keep her cool. "I know it's hard, but try to ignore it." Remind her that people aren't perfect and will mess up, and sometimes they mess up by saying untruthful things, sharing secrets, or being inconsiderate of others. Encourage her to choose what she shares with her friends carefully. Only time and experience can tell us which friends are trustworthy. Lend her a sympathetic ear and reassure her that as quickly as the rumor spread, it will probably cease.

If, however, the rumor is truly of a seriously damaging nature, you may need to step in as a parent and address the problem with the teacher or with the parents of the children who are spreading unkind gossip.

Strategic Planning (Manipulation)

"Shell, can Michael come over today?" Austin asked, as we were standing in the school lobby ready to head home.

"Another day, honey."

"But I already told him he could, and his mom said yes."

It's a game of "Gotcha!" I learned quickly. Now the rule is that only parents and nannies arrange playdates, and if I get put on the spot, the automatic answer is no.

Here's another example of strategic planning—a true story.

"Shell, can I bring my Game Boy to school?"

"No, sweetie, that's for home," I reply.

Then I see him whispering sweet nothings into his mom's ear as she asks aloud, "Did you already ask Shell?" The child, caught red-handed in the game of pitting nanny against mom, turned bright red and immediately sent himself to time-out.

In my experience, kids will attempt to strategically plan events that will get them what they want. Precious as they are, our darlings can also be amazingly sneaky and underhanded in plotting to get what they want, when they want it.

When my friend's son asked her for something he wanted and she said no, he had a habit of going elsewhere until he got the yes he was looking for. (He could have written the best-selling business book *Getting to Yes*.) When she said no on one occasion (probably to his request for a third cookie), he went across the street and asked the neighbor for one! You've got to hand it to him; he was persistent. In the above scenario, his mom and dad teamed up, and when the plot was uncovered, the child lost the privilege he wanted, for that day and for the day after.

There's nothing as awkward as being put on the spot by your own child. Sometimes children will carry out a plot between the two of them. I've been in situations where each one tells their mother or nanny that the other one agreed to the request, and both are simply hoping no one catches on!

Kids know the words that can get to a parent's heart: "You are so mean!" Don't be manipulated. You know what's best for your child, so have faith in your parenting skills and your years of wisdom, and don't look back.

Testing

"Do you think Mom will really send me to bed if I sneak a Popsicle after dinner?" "Do you think she really means it when she says that we can only watch PBS Kids?" From the get-go, it is important to have clear-cut boundaries and a commitment to consistently enforcing them. If you don't, your child will constantly push to see how far he can stretch your limits.

If the rule is that you are done eating for the night after your teeth are brushed, and your child sneaks a Popsicle, you should have a consequence for the behavior. He knew the rule, but he consciously broke it to see what you would do. That is testing. You don't want to disappoint him with the wrong answer!

"If you run off in the store one more time, we are leaving." Most likely he'll do it again to see if you mean what you say and say what you mean. It only takes once to follow through, and your child will quickly catch on that you mean business.

Expect many such "exams"—to test the boundaries—in the years to come.

Unloving Words

"I hate you." "You stink." "You are the worst mom ever!" We've all heard (or will hear) these at one time or another, usually as a result of a child not getting her way. I feel I've found the perfect remedy for when such comments come my way.

"Wow, I am sorry that you feel that way. Those words hurt because I love you so much." She can't argue with that; she can't give a comeback line. It ends the conversation right there. You are acknowledging that you are hearing her words, which hopefully means that she won't continually repeat them, and you are expressing your feelings to her.

With this response, you are eliminating the emotions she was hoping to stir up in you. (Guilt, guilt, and more guilt, followed by your contrite change of heart.) You are modeling an appropriate way to respond to someone who hurts your feelings, but you aren't giving in to her manipulation. If she continues to spout hateful and unloving words, remind her that you have heard her and have shared your thoughts, so the discussion is over. Remind her that her disrespectful attitude is enough to take away a privilege and that if she continues, you will do exactly that.

Again, there is a fine line between allowing your child to express her frustration and emotions, and her being disrespectful. You are going to have to draw that line based on your individual relationship with each child. If you have a child who is normally very respectful but all of a sudden has an out-of-character fit of rage, chances are that something is really bothering her and she needs your help to work through it. If unkind dramatics are a common pattern of behavior, it may be a good idea to have a "no tolerance" policy for unloving words as part of your family code.

Violence

"He punched me first. She pulled my hair!" In today's world, there is no escaping exposure to violence. It is in the media, in the schools, in the neighborhoods, and at childhood sporting events. True story: One little girl reported to her grandfather that a boy at school was pulling her hair in class. "What did you do?" her granddad asked. With hands on her kindergarten hips, she said, in no uncertain terms, "I told him to *stop* the violence!"

You gotta laugh, but this little gal was onto something. Violence starts with "stinking thinking" and gradually builds upon itself if not stopped, firmly, it its path.

Of course, the first line of defense against aggressive behavior is for you and your spouse to model a better way of handling frustrations and problems. If you or your spouse has an anger problem, please, please do the most loving thing for your child and take an anger-management class. If you don't get control of your temper, your child is doomed to repeat the pattern. But if you can demonstrate that you are willing to get help for a tendency to react in hurtful ways to others, what a gift you will give your kids! Most people who are violent saw violence in their homes. And as often as we tell ourselves, "I'll be different when I'm a mom" or, "I'll never do this to my kid when I'm a dad," we tend to repeat in knee-jerk style what we saw as kids, unless we are proactive and get help to make permanent changes.

Spousal abuse and child abuse are two of the most common and hidden dangers in American homes today. Typically we think of an abusive father, but if you have small children and a short fuse, you've probably realized that motherhood can bring out the monster in you. If you, as a mother, have a tendency to scream, yell, or hit your children in anger, I highly recommend Julie Barnhill's book *She's Gonna Blow!* available from Julie's Web site (www.juliebarnhill.com).[6]

For your child's protection, teach him to use his words as his first line of defense. "Stop! No! I don't like that!" is my favorite. Encourage your child to speak up when something is bothering him or someone is treating him in a way he doesn't like. If he can't resolve the situation on his own, reassure him that it is OK to get help from a teacher or parent.

I personally have a rule that we don't play with weapons. I just don't see the benefit in pretending to hurt others, so we skip that form of play. Use your influence to instill in your children your morals and values about respecting other people in everyday situations. Kids pick up on whether or not their parents live lives of general kindness. If you are kind to others—the homeless, animals, old and young, the vulnerable and weak—your child, I can almost guarantee, will adopt your empathetic spirit. There's no better antidote to violence than replacing such thoughts and actions with ones of kindness and tolerance.

Now the controversial topic. Should your child ever fight back? It is my personal opinion that children should never throw the first punch, but if they need to protect themselves, they should. This is a touchy subject because there is a potential to communicate mixed signals. I have found it beneficial to enroll my charges in a self-defense or karate class. It has taught them the importance of using their words as their first line of defense and has set clear-cut boundaries on when you should protect yourself and what level of protection you should use. For example, if a child is holding you by the arm, it would be better to twist out of the hold than to punch him in the face. There are many varieties of self-defense classes, and you can probably find one in your area that would fit your child's schedule and your religious preferences.

Whining

"Moooomeeeeee! Get me a pencil! I want a pencil like George's!" "Daaaadeeeeee, he got two cookies and I only got one!" Argh. The constant drip of a whiny child is like Chinese water torture. Here are some rules for winning the whining battle.

Never give in to whining or pleading. Tell your child, "If you use an appropriate voice, I will listen." Ignore the behavior until it stops.

Model what you'd like to hear. Say, "I don't understand the dramatic language you are using. It would be more effective to say, 'Mom, I can't find a pencil. Can you help me, please?'"

Model what you don't like to hear. Show, rather than tell, her how annoying it is. "Bella, I reeeeeeeeaaaaaaaaly want you to stoooooooop whining, puuuuhhhhhh-leeeeeeeaaaaaaasssssse!" If your child is whining constantly, you might even be able to record her and play back her voice so she can hear for herself how silly and obnoxious her whining is.

And most important, praise your child when she uses appropriate words in an appropriate voice.

X-Rays

"Ouch! That hurt!" your child screams as she takes a fall from a six-foot playground platform. Most kids I have known have had their share of bumps and bruises during their elementary-school years, myself included. I remember hanging upside down off the monkey bars in first grade and falling face-first with my teeth going through my front bottom lip. I still have the scar to prove it!

You will likely have to take your child to the hospital or minor emergency clinic at least a couple of times during the grade-school years, especially if your child is a boy (or a rambunctious, outgoing girl) and if you have more than two kids. Hospital visits are no fun, but I learned when Fraser broke his collarbone, by literally tripping while he was walking, that a calm and positive attitude can go a long way.

Generally, I don't run right over to my charge who has fallen down. I like to gauge his reaction based on his pain response, rather than on how he is seeing me react. I can get a much clearer picture of the extent of the injury. Stay calm and confident, and do what you have to do.

Many of today's hospitals have wonderful children's rooms filled with videos, games, and other distractions that make it seem almost as if you are on a romp at Chuck E. Cheese. Pediatric doctors and nurses know how to deal with a child who is frightened and injured. We've come a long way, baby, in caring for children— from those frightening experiences in cold hospital rooms that most of us experienced in our childhood. In fact, if you've not already done so, be sure to visit your local doctor's offices and hospitals and choose the ones that are the most child friendly—just in case your child breaks an arm or twists an ankle. You'll feel better being prepared.

Keeping current in first aid and CPR certification has given me the confidence and training to handle an emergency. I think it's great if parents (and grandparents, if they watch your children) also invest the time in learning these basics—doing so will help keep calm during the chaos.

Yelling

"MOOOOOM!" comes your child's bloodcurdling cry. You run down the hall expecting to see blood or the roof caved in on her. You arrive, breathless, at your child's door, and she sweetly asks, "Um, do we have any construction paper?"

Does your kid have only one volume—loud? Does everything from a hangnail to a stubbed toe constitute an emergency for her? So that you won't have a heart attack, it is important to teach kids about the volume of their voices and when it is OK to yell and when they simply need to come to you with their injury or other request.

When my charges' volume goes up, mine goes way down—almost to a whisper. "Boys, we need to use our indoor voice." They are usually quick to comply. If they have lots of energy and need to let it out, outside they go, where they can hoot and holler all they like.

If yelling has become your kids' default tone, work with them on practicing their indoor voices. You can insist that your kids get off of their seats and walk toward where you can hear them, rather than putting up with loud cries of "MOOOOOM!" all day long. (They've learned that you will have to put down what you are doing to come and hear them, when it really should be the other way around if they want your attention.)

My mom is hard of hearing, so my natural speaking tone is about ten times louder than most others', because I had to compensate for my mom not hearing me. It takes awhile for new people to realize that I'm not yelling on purpose, and I have to be respectful about lowering my tone. I've worked on it over the years and now have an appropriate indoor voice that I use rather nicely, most of the time.

When a child has an ear infection, blocked ears, or a hearing issue, they also will naturally speak more loudly. If your child tends to be a nonemotional yeller, meaning that her default voice is abnormally loud, mention it to your pediatrician and ask if having a hearing test may be worthwhile.

Zoolike Behavior

"Augh! Aaaaaa!" Just this morning when I came into work, I thought I had made a wrong turn and ended up at the zoo. Two off-the-wall kids were literally jumping on the couches, rolling on the floor, and making primatelike screeching noises. I made a note in my nanny diary:

December 5, 2005. Lesson learned. Tell Mom that kids will *not* be having Pop-Tarts for breakfast anymore.

Sometimes the energy level children have is amazing. It is important to provide adequate opportunities for them to let it all out. Sports, swimming, outdoor time, daily walks, and any other activity that involves releasing large amounts of energy at once are good things for elementary-school children.

For the most part, children's days are spent sitting in chairs, focusing on lessons. They wake up, get ready for school, go to school, sit at school, and then come home. That is almost nine hours with no real time to let their bodies run, jump, and stretch.

I suggest that every day you make some time for active activities. Whether it is indoor calisthenics, outdoor races, walking the dog, or any other form of exercise, children need the emotional break and the physical outlet to get rid of pent-up energy. If you join them, you, too, will get in on the benefits. You'll get in better shape and have some stress-relieving fun of hiking, playing shoot the hoops, or biking together to the store.

WRAP UP!

Bravo on braving it through to the end! If you've finished this book, you are well on your way to being your own Mary Poppins, whom Bert describes in the movie as "practically perfect in every way." Well, at least you're on your way to being as perfect as any parent (or nanny) could ever be.

I know there was a lot to digest in these pages, and like a spoonful of sugar, I hope the stories along with my tried-and-true nanny tips (plus a few from other experts and moms) helped the parenting medicine go down just a wee bit tastier. Keep this book handy, because your child's needs will change as he grows, and a chapter that didn't apply today may be just what you need in a few months.

As I wrote this book, the winds did indeed change direction, and I myself had to transition from my comfy world into a new one. Although the boys who were my charges for more than seven years are now half the country away, our love remains—as do the life lessons that we shared. We talk weekly and write letters, and I still get a chuckle over the interesting things that they "can't wait to tell me." During our first phone call, Austin was gleefully delighted that he *had* to do something inappropriate and it wasn't his fault. "Shell, you won't believe it. The school made me ride in a bus with no seat belts. How inappropriate was that? Should you call them?"

Fraser didn't understand why he "was being babied." "Shell, don't they know I am almost seven? I can do most things on my own!" The boys ask about my new charges and want to know if they are picky eaters and if they "do appropriate behavior." These stories and questions made me smile. Once again, I was reminded that although my job with Austin and Fraser is finished, the impact that I made on the kids will last a lifetime.

I take delight in knowing that within a very few weeks into my new nanny position, I've already bonded with the family and am making a positive contribution.

For someone who doesn't like change, I've adjusted quite well. I have been blessed with a family who welcomes me as a member of their parenting team.

Of course, there were emotional bumps along the road as I transitioned from one family to another, but I survived and learned a lot through the process. I admit there were times when I had to go back and look in my own first book to reassure myself that I was doing things right. I gleaned again, from the pages of my own writing, what I hope to impart to you—the confidence to be the best parent (or nanny) you can be. (I found rereading *Nanny to the Rescue!* equal to giving myself my very own, long, personal pep talk!)

I've started a new nanny diary for this new family. I'll share with you one of my first entries:

Day 12: Mom laughed when I told her how I called out for Sammy and he replied, "I'm in here in time-out!" In just days he had gone from not knowing what a time-out was, to putting himself there because he "used his hands instead of his words" when roughhousing with his sister.

Whew, I still have it.

RECOMMENDED READING

In addition to the books I've recommended throughout this book, you may want to check out these additional resources. But remember: just as no parent can be perfect, no parenting resource can be either. Take what you like, and throw away the rest.

Badegruber, Bernie. *101 Life Skills Games for Children: Learning, Growing, Getting Along (Ages 6–12).* Alameda, CA: Hunter House, 2004.

Borba, Michele. *Don't Give Me That Attitude! 24 Rude, Selfish, Insensitive Things Kids Do and How to Stop Them.* New York: Jossey-Bass, 2004.

Campbell, Ross. *How to Really Parent Your Child: Anticipating What a Child Needs Instead of Reacting to What a Child Does.* Nashville: W Publishing Group, 2005.

Drescher, John M. *When Your Child Is 6 to 12.* New York: Good Books, 2001.

Durbin, Kara. *Parenting with Scripture: A Topical Guide for Teachable Moments.* Chicago: Moody, 2001.

Hart, Dr. Archibald D. *Helping Children Survive Divorce.* Nashville: W Publishing Group, 1997.

Johnson, Dr. Matthew A. *Positive Parenting with a Plan (Grades K–12): F.A.M.I.L.Y. Rules.* New York: Publication Consultants, 2002.

Kimmel, Tim. *Grace-Based Parenting.* Nashville: W Publishing Group, 2005.

Latham, Glenn I. *Christlike Parenting: Taking the Pain Out of Parenting.* Detroit: Gold Leaf Press, 1999.

————. *The Power of Positive Parenting: A Wonderful Way to Raise Children.* North Logan, UT: P & T Ink, 1994.

Leman, Kevin. *Single Parenting That Works.* Wheaton, IL: Tyndale, 2006.

MacArthur, John. *Successful Christian Parenting.* Nashville: W Publishing Group, 1999.

Munger, Richard L. *Changing Children's Behavior by Changing the People, Places and Activities in Their Lives.* Boys Town, NE: Boys Town Press, 2005.

Pantley, Elizabeth. *Perfect Parenting.* New York: McGraw-Hill, 1998.

Phelan, Thomas. *1-2-3 Magic: Effective Discipline for Children 2–12.* 3rd ed. Glen Ellyn, IL: ParentMagic, 2003.

Stanley, Charles F. *How to Keep Your Kids on Your Team.* Nashville: Thomas Nelson, 2004.

NOTES

Introduction

1. Michelle LaRowe, *Nanny to the Rescue! Straight Talk and Super Tips for Parenting in the Early Years* (Nashville: W Publishing Group, 2006).

Chapter 2—Where Did *That* Come From?

1. See Ephesians 4:15.

2. John Eldredge, *Wild at Heart: Discovering the Secret of a Man's Soul* (Nashville: Thomas Nelson, 2001).

Chapter 4—The Great School Debate

1. Teresa Méndez, "Public Schools: Do They Outperform Private Ones?" *Christian Science Monitor*, May 10, 2005, http://www.csmonitor.com/2005/0510/p11s01-legn.html.

2. Teresa Méndez, "Public School Tops Private in Test," *Christian Science Monitor*, May 10, 2005, http://www.cbsnews.com/stories/2005/05/10/national/main694303.shtml.

3. Ibid.

4. Dr. Brian Ray, "Facts on Homeschooling," National Home Education Research Institute, http://www.nheri.org/facts-on-homeschooling.html.

5. America's Charter School Finance Corporation, "The Charter School Experience," 2002, http://www.charterfriends.org/Charter_School_Experience.pdf.

6. Education Commission of the States, "Charter Schools," http://www.ecs.org/html/issue.asp?issueID=20.

Chapter 6—Planning Perfect Playdates

1. Proverbs 27:17.

Chapter 7—Playground Politics and Personality Conflicts

1. Matthew 5:9, emphasis added.

2. Gary Smalley and John Trent, *The Two Sides of Love* (Colorado Springs: Focus on the Family, 1999).

Chapter 8—Friendship Factors

1. Proverbs 18:24, YLT

Chapter 9—Taking a Bite out of Bullying

1. Kentucky Youth Anti-Bullying Alliance, "Why Kentucky's Kids Need HB 270," http://www.kyyouth.org/Publications/HB%20270%20 talking%20points%20bullying%20handout%20rev%2001%2017%20% 202006.pdf.

2. Richard B. Goldbloom, Dr., "Parents' Primer on School Bullying," *Reader's Digest* special feature, http://www.readersdigest.ca/ mag/2001/10/bullying.html.

3. David L. Silvernail, "A Survey of Bullying Behavior Among Maine Third Graders," University of Southern Maine, 2000, http://lincoln. midcoast.com/~wps/against/finalreport.html.

4. Kids Health for Parents, "Dealing with Bullying," http://www.kidshealth. org/teen/your_mind/problems/bullies.html.

Chapter 10—The Thrill of Victory and the Agony of Defeat

1. See Proverbs 22:6.

Chapter 12—Allowance, Chores, and Other Money Matters

1. Christine Field, *Life Skills for Kids* (Colorado Springs: Shaw, 2000).

Chapter 13—What's Happening to My Body?

1. Annette Smith, *Help! My Little Boy's Growing Up* (Eugene, OR: Harvest House, 2002).

2. This list is adapted from Becky Freeman, *Mom's Everything Book for Daughters* (Grand Rapids: Zondervan, 2003).

3. Abigail H. Natenshon, *When Your Child Has an Eating Disorder: A Step-by-Step Workbook for Parents and Other Caregivers* (New York: Jossey Bass, 1999).

4. Nancy Rue, *The Body Book—It's a God Thing!* (Grand Rapids: Zonderkidz, 2000).

5. Smith, *Help! My Little Boy's Growing Up.*

6. This list is adapted from Becky Freeman, *Mom's Everything Book for Sons* (Grand Rapids: Zondervan, 2003).

7. William Pollock, *Real Boys: Rescuing Our Sons from the Myths of Boyhood* (New York: Random House, 1998), 102.

8. Ibid.

9. Ibid.

Chapter 14—Virtues to Grow On

1. Frederic Luskin, *Forgive for Good* (San Francisco: HarperSanFrancisco, 2001).

2. Luke 10:25–37.

3. 1 Timothy 3:6 TLB.

4. Colossians 3:23.

Michelle's Problemossary

1. 2 Thessalonians 3:10 TLB.

2. Victorian Curriculum and Assessment Authority, "Social, Emotional, and Cognitive Development and Its Relationship to Learning in School Prep to Year 10," http://72.14.203.104/search?q=cache:sWGLDYtxYxMJ:vels.vcaa. vic.edu.au/downloads/discusspapers/socialdeveloplearning.pdf+stamford+ marshmallow+study&hl=en&gl=us&ct=clnk&cd=4.

3. Ibid.

4. Gary Chapman, *The Five Love Languages of Children* (Chicago: Moody, 1997).

5. Ephesians 4:32.

6. Julie Barnhill, *She's Gonna Blow!* (Eugene, OR: Harvest House, 2005).

To find out more about Michelle LaRowe or read additional nanny tips, visit www.michellelarowe.com.

ABOUT THE AUTHOR

Michelle LaRowe is "America's Nanny" and author of *Nanny to the Rescue!* The 2004 International Nanny Association "Nanny of the Year" and a credentialed career nanny for twelve years, Michelle is the founder and president of Boston Area Nannies, Inc., vice president of the International Nanny Association, and a proud member of Christian Nannies.

www.michellelarowe.com

Printed in the USA
CPSIA information can be obtained
at www.ICGtesting.com
LVHW080749050824
787165LV00006B/12

9 780849 912443